بسم الله الرحمن الرحيم

In the Name of Allah, the Most Generous, the Most Merciful

Prayer

Ayatollah Sayyid Fadhel Hosseini Milani

ISLAM IN
ENGLISH
PRESS

ISLAM IN ENGLISH PRESS

First published in Great Britain in 2011 by Islam in English Press

A CIP catalogue record for this book can be found in The British Library.

ISBN 978-0-9541585-4-5

Islam in English Press
P.O. Box 2842, London W6 9ZH

Printed and bound in Great Britain by CPI Antony Rowe

ISLAM IN ENGLISH PRESS
for accessible guides to Islamic knowledge

Contents

Introduction vi

The significance of prayer 1

Introduction to prayer 3

Why we pray 10

Purity of body and soul 14

Obligatory prayers 17

Voluntary prayers 49

Introduction

Considered to be the pillar of religion, prayer characterizes Muslim life.

While those who stand in prayer are showered with Allah's mercy and surrounded by Angels, one of their number remarks, 'If people comprehended the extent of its benefit, their prayer would be endless.'

The Messenger of Allah ﷺ likened prayer to the availability of a hot bath tub, that when used five times a day removes ingrained and surface dirt.

This work attempts to provide a precise clarification of prayer and all the rulings that cover this important subject

Prayer

The significance of prayer

Qur'ānic āyat on the significance of prayer

1. Maintain prayer at both ends of the day — and the early hours of night. For it is through good deeds that bad deeds are effaced.
   Qur'ān 11:114

2. He is glorified in the morning and the evening by those — not distracted from remembrance of Allāh by bargain or trade — who maintain the prayer and give *zakāh*. For they fear a day in which hearts and sights are transformed.
   Qur'ān 24:37

3. Allāh will surely help those who help Him. For Allāh is All-Powerful, Almighty. If We would grant them power over the land they would maintain the prayer, give *zakāh*, enjoin what is right and forbid what is wrong — for the outcome of all matters rests with Allāh.
   Qur'ān 22:40–41

4. Certainly, it is the faithful who attain salvation — those who are humble in prayer and baulk at all conceit.
   Qur'ān 23:1–3

The significance of prayer from Nahj al-Balāghah

1. Commit yourself to maintain prayer. Offer them as frequently as possible in order to seek nearness to Allāh. For prayer casts off sin as trees do their leaves. The Messenger of Allāh ﷺ likened it to the availability of a hot bath that, used five times a day, cleanses one of all dirt.
   Sermon 199

2. For the God-fearing, prayer is the means by which to seek closeness to Allāh.
   Maxim 136

3. Keep Allāh in mind apropos the Qur'ān. No one should excel you in acting upon it.

   Keep Allāh in mind apropos prayer, because it is the pillar of your religion.

   Keep Allāh in mind apropos Your Lord's House [Kaʿbah], do not forsake it while you remain alive . . .
   Imām ʿAlī's last words to his sons

4. Sleep, in a state of firm belief, is better than prayer in a state of doubt.
   Imām ʿAlī's comment at seeing a Khārijite offering the midnight prayer

Imām Ṣādiq ؑ on the significance of prayer

1. When people stand for prayer Allāh's mercy rains down upon them. Angels surround them as one of their number comments, 'If people comprehended the full benefit of prayer, their prayers would never cease.'
   Wasa'il al-Shiʿah, Vol. 4, p.32

2. When anyone praised another in the presence of Imām Ṣādiq ؑ, his sole interest was to know about her/his prayer.
   Wasa'il al-Shiʿah, Vol. 4, p.32

3. Prayer may be likened to a tent pole that is maintained in an upright position by guy-ropes and tent pegs. However, if the pole breaks, neither ropes nor pegs are able to afford it further support.
   Wasa'il al-Shiʿah, Vol. 4, p. 33

(All quotations attributed to any of the 12 error-free Imāms of the progeny of Allāh's Holy Messenger ﷺ refer to what was said by the Messenger of Allāh ﷺ himself.)

Introduction to prayer

All of us are able to exercise and develop our muscles. Some do so to keep fit, some to participate in a particular sport and others to shape and sculpt their bodies. Whatever our motive, success is only achieved by way of sustained application and effort. This applies equally to intellectual development, with academic qualifications being awarded after years of diligent study, and, it follows, to the development of our innate spiritual capacities.

While it is apparent that the body requires nourishment, care and protection to grow and flourish, precious few consider the soul's need for similar nourishment, care, protection and growth. As though bedazzled by the 'limousine' that they are happy to refill, wash and securely house, many appear blind to the 'essence' of the entity it carries through this life. Like children who do not understand that education is an investment for the future, they do not grasp that this material world affords the soul the opportunity to realize its true potential and achieve its objective. They are able to register and respond to stimuli that materially affect their 'world-space' or 'worldview' but, as spiritual life does not exist for them, they are not able to register or respond to spiritual stimuli. For similar reasons, a pack of wild wolves only equipped to register other creatures as potential meals is not able to register and respond to stimuli — such as status, gold ornaments or 'state-of-the-art' electronic equipment — that for them do not exist in any meaningful sense.

However, the fact that, to some people, a thing may seem not to exist does not prove that it is in fact non-existent. During routine eye tests those with astigmatism are often surprised to perceive details not previously apparent to them, as are those with stereopsis when enabled to see with full three-dimensional vision. And, although it may stare them in the face, those who are 'colour blind' do not see numerals formed by tonal dots within fields of similarly toned coloured dots.

To some extent, lack of awareness may also result from upbringing, as William Wordsworth — appointed Poet Laureate in 1843 — expresses so beautifully in these few lines from his ode, *Intimations of Immortality*,

> The Soul that rises with us, our life's Star, Hath had elsewhere its setting, And cometh from afar;
>
> Not in entire forgetfulness, And not in utter nakedness, but trailing clouds of glory do we come from God, who is our home:
>
> Heaven lies about us in our infancy! Shades of the prison-house begin to close upon the growing boy,
>
> But he beholds the light, and whence it flows, he sees it in his joy;
>
> The Youth who daily farther from the east must travel, still is Nature's priest and by the vision splendid, is on his way attended;
>
> At length the Man perceives it die away, and fade into the light of common day.
>
> Earth fills her lap with pleasures of her own; Yearnings she hath in her own natural kind,
>
> And, even with something of a mother's mind, and no unworthy aim, the homely nurse doth all she can to make her foster-child, her inmate Man, forget the glories he hath known, and that imperial palace whence he came. . . .
>
> Thou little Child, yet glorious in the might of heaven-born freedom on thy being's height,
>
> Why with such earnest pains dost thou provoke the years to bring the inevitable yoke, thus blindly with thy blessedness at strife?
>
> Full soon thy soul shall have her earthly freight, and custom lie upon thee with a weight heavy as frost, and deep almost as life.

Despite this, the works of painters such as Edward Hopper eloquently illustrate the soul's yearning to transcend the mundane and emerge into celestial light.

Jallaludin Rumi also refers to this in his lines:

> Hearken to this Reed forlorn,
> Breathing, ever since was torn
> From its rushy bed,
> a strain of impassioned love and pain . . .
>
> **R. A. Nicholson, *Rumi Poet and Mystic*, redrafted by A. J. Arberry, Unwin Paperbacks 1978**

Having revealed the outward manifestations of the faith — its practical, ethical and social precepts — and having summoned humankind to His side, to His Inner Reality, Allāh Almighty has also provided a link between the outward aspects of faith and the position of the spirit. The only nourishment needed by a soul in order to hone its ability to see everything with the help of Allāh — 'Light of the Heavens and the Earth' — is 'communication with the Creator' who has granted each one the non-materialistic attribute referred to as the soul's 'eye'.

Thus, the objective of the inner and outward aspects of the faith of Islam extends beyond the life of this world. The term 'nearness to Allāh' stretches beyond physical nearness to the lords of wealth and power of this world, for those who step on the path of human destiny travel a straight path to 'Nearness to Ultimate Truth' — *Al-Ḥaqq*. Beings who exist in this world should not imagine that success is limited to excellence in the sciences, arts, skills, customs or traditions that confer status in society. Real success can only be achieved through the refinement of the soul, and appreciation that its ultimate goal is the Purified Essence of Unity.

Allāh gave the Prophet Muḥammad ﷺ access to His religious commandments and Divine precepts so that he ﷺ would focus our attention on the destination of this life's journey. He ﷺ taught us how these relate to our 'well-being' or 'wretchedness' in the next world; how the blessing of everlasting happiness is achieved by putting those Divine precepts into practice; how dedicated and determined effort brings us closer to Allāh; and how, at the higher stages of closeness, human spirituality may approach truth and reality.

Thus, to travel the 'Path to Nearness' is to tread the path of servitude, humility, self–annihilation and non–being rather than mastery over the things of this world. Those who travel this route are like jewels with Allāh's power and strength at their core.

This is the position that Allāh refers to in the Qur'ān when He talks about the Prophet Muḥammad ﷺ:

> Certainly you have in the Messenger of Allāh an excellent example for those who consistently remember Allāh and place their hope in Allāh and the Last Day.
> **Qur'ān 33:21**

> Say, if you love Allāh follow me; Allāh will love you and forgive you your sins . . .
> **Qur'ān 3:31**

In these *āyat*, the Prophet Muḥammad ﷺ is introduced as our exemplar for behaviour and morality — whose example we should take as our precedent. It evidences the Prophet's freedom from sin and error, for had this not been so, there would have been no value in Allāh Almighty presenting him as a leader and as a precedent. This position was passed from the Prophet ﷺ to his Household عليهم السلام, as is witnessed by *aḥadīth* reported by many scholars:

> I leave among you two precious things: the book of Allāh and my progeny. These two will not be separated until they meet together at the pool of Kawthar [in paradise]. Always follow them otherwise you will perish, and do not attempt to instruct them, for they are wiser than you.
> **Sunan of Abu Dāwūd**
> **Khasaʿis of Nisaʿi, p.30**
> **Ṣaḥiḥ of Muslim, Vol. 7, p.122**
> **Sunan of Tirmithi, Part 2, p.307**
> **Mustadrak of Ḥakim, Vol.3, pp.109 & 148**
> **Musnad of Ahmad ibn Ḥanbal, Vol.3, pp.14–17; Vol.4, pp.26 & 59; and Vol.5, pp.182 & 189**

The Prophet ﷺ said:

> I am the city of knowledge and ʿAlī is its gate; so whoever wants to enter the city should come through the gate.
> **Al-Ḥakim's Al-Mustadrak, Vol. 3, p.26**

Hubshi ibn Janadah reported that the Prophet ﷺ said:

> ʿAlī is from me and I am from ʿAlī and no one represents me but ʿAlī.
> **Sunan Ibn Majah, Vol. 1, Number 119**

The Prophet ﷺ said to ʿAlī, Faṭimah, Ḥasan and Ḥusayn عليهم السلام:

> I am at peace with those whom you are at peace with; and I am at war with those whom you are at war with.
> **Sunan Ibn Majah, Vol. 1, Number 145**

Abu Hurrairah reported that the Prophet ﷺ said:

> Whoever loves Ḥasan and Ḥusayn عليهما السلام loves me, and whoever hates them hates me.
> **Sunan Ibn Majah, Vol. 1, Number 143**

In the language of the Qur'ān, the holder of 'the degree of nearness' — the one who links humankind to its Inner Reality — is called *Imām*. It is therefore the Prophet ﷺ and error-free Imāms عليهم السلام who hold the reins of spiritual guidance on Allāh's behalf, who transmit the light of Allāh to our hearts.

> So believe in Allāh and His messenger and the light We have sent down . . .
> **Qur'ān 64:8**

From the *āyah* below it is clear that Allāh ordered the Prophet Muḥammad ﷺ to direct Muslims to establish a special closeness vis-à-vis his ﷺ progeny:

> Say [O Muḥammad]: I do not ask you for any reward [for the toils of Prophethood] but love of my progeny.
> **Qur'ān 42:23**

This facet of *wila* — closeness — that relates to his ﷺ progeny is reiterated in the *ḥadīth* of *Ghadīr Khum* in which the Prophet ﷺ said:

> For those of whom I am mawla [those over whom I have authority] ʿAli is also mawla.
> **Al-Amini's Al-Ghadīr, Vol.1, pp.14–18**

It also appears in the Qur'ānic *āyah*:

> Truly, truly, your guardian [waliy] is Allāh, His messenger [Muḥammad] and those who believe, establish the prayer, and give to the poor while they bow [in prayer].
> **Qur'ān 5:55**

No Muslim scholar understands this *āyah* to be a universal instruction for all Muslims to give *zakat* while in *rukūʿ*. Al-Ṭabari, Al-Zamakhshari and Fakhruʿd-Din āl-Rāzi clarified that 'pay *zakat* while they bow in prayer' refers specifically to the occasion on which, while, bent directly forwards from the waist during prayer — *rukūʿ* — 'Alī عليه السلام was asked for charity — and took off his ring and gave it. The revelation of this *āyah* identifies the specific person who, in addition to Allāh and His Messenger ﷺ, is the leader of the Muslims. Leader in this sense denotes 'guardian of', or 'one who has authority over the affairs of others . . .'

Another facet of closeness refers to the 'Wila of Love' — *maḥabbah* — and the 'Wila of Kinship' — *qarabah*. The 'Wila of Love' and the 'Wila of Kinship' indicate that people should cultivate love and closeness to the Prophet's progeny over and above the love and closeness they should have for other Muslims. Qur'ānic and *aḥadīth* references, narrated by all Muslim sources, confirm that love for the Prophet's progeny is a basic precept of Islam.

Every Islamic precept has an underlying philosophical and spiritual reason. The reason and benefit of the need to love and feel close to the Prophet's progeny عليهم السلام is that it is bonds of love that truly connect people to 'them'. It is those bonds that make people yearn to learn from them, to emulate their behaviour and manner, and to draw benefit from their purity and closeness to Allāh. Two famous scholars, Al-Zamakhshari and Fakhruʿd-Din al-Rāzi, both narrate the *ḥadīth* on the 'Wila of Love'. Al-Rāzi quoting al-Zamakhshari relates that the Prophet ﷺ said:

> Whoever dies while in love with the progeny of Muḥammad — has died a martyr;
>
> Whoever dies while in love with the progeny of Muḥammad — has died in forgiveness;
>
> Whoever dies while in love with the progeny of Muḥammad — has died a believer in the perfection of their faith.
>
> **Al-Tafsir al-Kabir, Al-Razi, Vol. 27, p.166**

Wila, in its sense of the Imāmate or leadership of the 12 error-free Imāms, is the position of authority in the faith to which matters are referred for decision. That is, it is a position that others should follow, should adopt as their example for action and behaviour, and from which they should learn the precepts of the faith. Such a position is necessarily one that is free from sin — *ʿiṣmah* — so that the speech and actions of such Imāms are safe guidance for others.

Thus, the 12 error-free Imāms of *Ahl al-Bayt* are acknowledged as the authoritative source of what the Prophet ﷺ said and did. Had they been associated with unrighteousness or ignorance, had they had ceased to be the complement of the Qur'ān, and had they not been, like the Prophet ﷺ himself, free from sin and error, they could not have been exemplars and leaders in the Prophet's place.

In the second year after the Prophet ﷺ had migrated to Madinah revelations established the

> Call to prayer — *athān*
>
> Mental and physical purification that conditions and readies one to commune with the Lord — *wuḍū'*,
>
> Mandatory prayers — *ṣalāt*, and
>
> Direction to face in order to align one's being with the earthly core of Islam — *qiblah*.

The Prophet Muḥammad ﷺ taught people how to pray — and this section is for those who seek to follow the path of servanthood taught by him ﷺ,

and who desire to adhere as accurately as is possible to his ﷺ teaching — for Allāh tells us in the Qur'ān,

> In Allāh's Messenger you certainly have an excellent example for those who place their hope in Allāh and the Last Day, and are constant in the remembrance of Allāh.
> **Qur'ān 33:21**

Allāh's final Prophet ﷺ departed this world in the year 11 AH at the age of 63.

Why we pray

> O you who believe! Seek help through patience and prayer . . .
> **Qur'ān 2:153**

The significance of prayer in our lives

As individuals

Prayer is the most highly esteemed communication between human beings and their Creator.

It develops our 'greatest faculty's' capacity for concentration — and evidences the highest level of submission to Allāh Almighty.

It purifies the soul and provides a framework for life's daily discipline — in particular, prayers offered at their specified times.

Prayer affords the satisfaction of having fulfilled daily obligations, and affords a spiritual taste of the sweetness of being in Allāh's presence.

Recitation and remembrance maintain 'Awareness of Allāh' and encourage perception of the — everywhere evident — 'signs' of His mercy and wisdom.

As families

As Islam's first preference is for prayer to be offered in a mosque, its second is for prayer to be offered in congregation, while prayer within the family has lesser significance. Nonetheless, parents have responsibility to encourage children to fulfil this most essential pillar of Islam. When toddlers watch parents perform *wuḍū'* and offer daily prayer, they inevitably copy them and adopt these practices.

As a community

Prayer strengthens bonds between community members who assemble to share common experiences five times a day (or three times — when *Ḍuḥr* and *ʿAṣr*, or *Maghrib* and *ʿIshā'*, are contiguously offered; ref. Qur'ān 17:78).

The community coheres and is unified by being together at the mosque.

As congregational prayers are often accompanied by discussions of Islamic rulings and lectures on the Qur'ān and *aḥadīth*, the educational value and influence of community prayer is compounded.

Mosques are not merely places of worship, but also places in which social problems are often solved, fellow Muslims consulted about community affairs and crucial decisions apropos the community determined.

As an ummah

Prayer increases awareness of the needs of the 'worldwide' *ummah*, for whose contentment Muslims pray.

All Muslims face one *qiblah*, communicate with the One Divinity — Allāh Almighty — and are all united by common goals and objectives.

Historical aspects of faith

The first prayer ever offered in Islam was when the Prophet Muḥammad ﷺ stood in the Holy Mosque of Makkah with Khadījah عليها السلام and the young boy ʿAlī عليه السلام behind him. From this event the apparent strength of Islam encouraged others to profess faith also. When the Prophet ﷺ migrated to Madinah his first action was to build a mosque. That mosque has remained the represen-tative symbol of Islamic heritage throughout the centuries.

The significance of prayer for Muslims today

As secularism offers no solution to spiritual problems, all the hopes, aspirations and prosperity of human beings rest with faith and regular communication between human beings and their Creator. Prayer plays a central role in uplifting the spiritual standing of humanity.

The ongoing relevance of discipline

Consistency and regularity of daily prayer contribute to discipline and organization — the secret of every success. For Muslims the discipline of prayer is as automatic as brushing the teeth — which similarly refreshes and contributes to feelings of 'well-being'. As with the brushing of teeth, rewards — although long-lasting — yield their benefits over time.

The ongoing relevance of unity

Congregational prayers at central mosques — to which all must travel — are effective in establishing unity amongst those who attend. This serves to crumble the artificial barriers of society, professions, wealth, class and neighbourhood, and to re-establish the equality of all human beings before Allāh.

The ongoing relevance of identity

Congregating with others strengthens the individual's identity as a component of a larger group — in the same way that supporters identify with their football team. In the Western world in particular, congregational prayers reinforce bonds and relationships with the worldwide Muslim *ummah*. During the last decades of the 20th century Muslims were accused of being terrorists and attacking civilization. The new century will, '*Inshā'a-Allāh*', witness the opposite and demonstrate the tolerance and broadmindedness of Muslims who participate and contribute to society — as their ancestors did. Politicians in the Western world have begun to realize this and to count on younger Muslims for positive contributions.

The fruits of remembrance

The essential teaching of Islam is to strive to feel the Omnipresence of Allāh during every single moment of life as the Qur'ān and 'Traditions' emphasize:

> Remembrance of Allāh satisfies the heart.
> **Qur'ān 13:28**

> Remembrance of Allāh illuminates the heart.
> **Ghorar al-Ḥikam**

> Remembrance of Allāh leads to the love of Allāh.
> **Biḥar al-Anwār, Vol. 93, p.160**

> Remembrance of Allāh is the key to prosperity.
> **Biḥar al-Anwār, Vol. 77, p.199**

> Remembrance of Allāh is nourishment for the soul.
> **Ghorar al-Ḥikam**

> Remembrance of Allāh is a cure.
> **Kanz al-Ummāl, Tradition 1751**

> Remembrance of Allāh keeps Shayṭān away.
> **Nahj al-Balāghah, Sermon No. 2**

> Remembrance of Allāh prevents hypocrisy.
> **Biḥar al-Anwār, Vol. 77, p.290**

Remembrance of Allāh's omnipresence inspires people and effectively deters them from succumbing to temptations and doing wrong.

The disadvantage of neglecting to remember Allāh

Some advantages of the remembrance of Allāh, essential elements in the building of Islamic personality, are listed above and some consequences of the failure to remember Him are listed below:

> The lives of those who turn from My remembrance will be circumscribed and they shall be raised blind on the Day of Judgement.
> **Qur'ān 20:124**

> We will appoint a devil as intimate companion of those who withdraw themselves from the remembrance of The Most Gracious.
> **Qur'ān 43:36**

> Shayṭān plans to create hostility and hatred between you, and to use intoxicants and gambling to hinder your remembrance of Allāh.
> **Qur'ān 5:91**

It is not those who leave art exhibitions with blurred memories of pretty pictures who appreciate or understand the stature and achievement of an artist. It is those who grasp the significance, and appreciate the artist's achievement, who in reality understand and esteem the artist's work. And it is only those of us who grasp the significance of the signs of creation in the heavens and the earth, who genuinely glorify Allāh Almighty and remember Him.

Purity of body and soul

The manufacture of detergents and cleaning materials is a highly profitable business. Millions are spent on advertising soaps, shampoos, conditioners, washing powders etc. Families that maintain clean, wholesome and healthy homes also ensure that their bodies, clothing, bed linen, soft furnishings and houses are kept clean. That cleanliness is of the utmost importance is illustrated by a tradition of Allāh's final Messenger ﷺ in which he said, 'Cleanliness is part of faith.' The question is — why do we assume such traditions refer only to bodily cleanliness when purification of the soul is the very objective of our existence?

Many *āyat* of the Qur'ān refer to purification of the soul as the essential element in the attainment of prosperity, see Qur'ān 91:9 and 87:14. This is realized in two ways — one positive, one negative. The negative is to keep away from sin, the positive is to pray.

A 'true believer' may achieve inner wisdom and knowledge of spiritual truths through her/his inner heart. The heart and 'inner heart' are closely linked. The difference between them is that the heart 'knows' while the inner heart 'sees'. When knowledge and vision combine, the unseen becomes visible and certainty is achieved. This was the goal of the Prophet Ibrāhīm عليه السلام when he saw the '*Malakūt*' of the heavens and the earth referred to in Qur'ān 6:75. There is no point in knowledge without vision, nor in vision without knowledge. It is analogous to visiting a foreign country without understanding its language, history or customs.

The Prophet ﷺ said,

> Worship Allāh as if you see Him for even if you do not, He truly sees you.
>
> **Biḥar al-Anwār, Vol. 77, p. 74**

Once, when the Prophet ﷺ explained the significance of daily prayer to his companions, he asked, 'Do you think traces of filth adhere to the body of a person who has a flowing spring at the entrance to his house and is able to wash five times a day?' His companions thought not. He ﷺ continued, 'In like manner, the five daily prayers remove dirt, filth, corruption and uncleanness from souls.'

When we have decided where we want to go, and have agreed to adhere to the regulations that govern that course, we may become comfortably established — in the 'carriage' of prayer — and be transported to our destination as it travels.

The heart's presence during prayer

Prayer is a celestial formula and 'Divine Electuary'. Every part contains a hidden 'Mystery'. Prayer is an expression of love, communication, and remembrance of the Lord of the Universe. It is the most excellent channel for spiritual perfection, ascension, and nearness to Allāh. In one tradition, prayer is referred to as being the believer's 'Heavenly Journey' — *Miʿrāj*.

Prayer is such a pure sparkling stream of spirituality that those who enter it five times a day purify their souls of every category of pollution and contamination. It is the key aspect for Allāh Almighty and is the criterion for acceptance of all other deeds and acts of worship. However, none of the above advantages, or fruits of prayer, are achieved without the heart being present — that is, without devoting its full attention to Allāh Almighty with utmost humbleness.

All the elements of prayer — *wuḍū'*, invocations, recitals of Qur'ānic *āyat*, bowing with deference, prostration in submission, bearing witness and salutation — constitute the 'face and body' of the prayer, while the heart's presence and attention to the Creator express its 'spirit'. Just as a body without a spirit is acknowledged to be dead, prayer that is offered without the heart's presence — even though it might satisfy the performance of an obligatory act of worship — does not contribute to the achievement of any higher spiritual position. Allāh tells us in the Qur'ān,

> Establish Worship for My Remembrance.
> **Qur'ān 20:14**

The Friday prayer has been described as an invocation:

> O you who believe, when the call for the prayer on Friday is heard, hasten to the remembrance of Allāh.
> **Qur'ān 57:9**

In one tradition the Prophet ﷺ emphasized the above saying,

> Sometimes only half a prayer is accepted — at others, possibly only a third, a quarter, or a tenth — while some prayers, like crumpled clothes thrown by a careless child, are completely rejected.
> **Biḥar al-Anwār, Vol. 84. p.260**

The link between remembrance and prayer

Remembrance of Allāh — *Dhikr Allāh* — is evidenced by the heart, by the tongue and by the limbs and — when all are combined altogether in a single communication with Allāh Almighty — by *ṣalāt*.

How to obtain the spiritual advantages of ṣalāt

The Prophet ﷺ showed his companions how to pray and ordered them to follow his example. He ﷺ, his progeny عليهم السلام and his faithful companions then initiated them into how to derive the utmost spiritual advantage from prayer. They highly recommended the following:

1. To remind oneself that the prayer being offered might be our final one. The effect is to increase the intensity of concentration in the hope that the maximum benefit from this opportunity is achieved.

2. To intend to express the utmost submission and humility during prayer. None are able to 'draw close' to Allāh Almighty until they are aware and have accepted that they themselves are insignificant creatures. The Prophet ﷺ once commented on the carelessness of someone who was praying, saying, 'Had he been truly humble he would have remained aware of the awesomeness of his communication and been more measured in his actions.'

3. To understand, while declaring *Allāhu Akbar*, that He is far greater than these words are able to express. Alternately, to have consciously and sincerely placed one's absolute reliance on the Greatest and Mightiest Power.

4. To manifest during bowing with deference — *rukūʿ* — absolute faith and total submission, regardless of whether He should decide to behead you or not.

5. While in prostration — *sujud* — to concentrate on the fact that we have been created from earth, are returned to it by burial and will, on the Day of Judgement, be again raised from it.

6. It is highly recommended: while standing upright, for eyes to be focused on the point where the forehead will meet the earth; while bowing with deference, for eyes to be focused between one's feet; while sitting between prostrations and while bearing witness — *tashahud* — for eyes to be focused on one's lap; and while offering the invocation — *qunūt* — for eyes to be focused on the palms of one's hands.

7. It is also highly recommended that the nose touch the earth during prostration. In many traditions this act is expressed as defiance to Shayṭān — his intention being to divert submission from Allāh — for this act is an expression of utter submission to Him.

8. And, when raising hands to the ears and uttering *Allāhu Akbar,* to be conscious of surrender to Supreme Authority; when standing upright, to relax the arms with palms in contact with the thighs; when in prostration, for males to keep hands directed inwards and elbows outward — forming the arms into 'wings', *tajniḥ* — and for females, to keep hands pointing forwards with elbows close to their sides.

   Al-Kāfi, Vol. 3, pp. 310–363

How to pray

There are three aspects to discuss: how to prepare for worship; conditions to be complied with during worship; and the the offering of the prayer. In addition, some prayers are obligatory while others are voluntary.

Obligatory prayers

Preparation

This includes:
Ablution, ablution with water — *wuḍū'* and *ghusl*, and ablution when water is not available — *tayamum*.

Wuḍū'

The Arabic word used in aḥadīth references — *wuḍū'* — cleanliness, encompasses mental as well as physical cleansing. When used as a technical term, it refers to 'preparation for worship'. This, when done in a quiet prayerful manner, is regarded as being a part of the act of worship.

Requirements of *wuḍū'*

- The following presumes that hands, face, head and feet are physically clean and free from impurity.
- Specific intention to achieve closeness with Allāh Almighty. Thus, if the actions of *wuḍū'* are done for any reason other than this, they are not considered suitable preparation for an act of worship.
- To rinse hands and the face, pour a little water into the cupped hands and, with the right-hand palm drawn in a downward movement, clean the face from the hairline to the extremity of the beard. The area required to be cleansed is the distance between the end of the extended thumb and end of the extended middle finger. To ensure that the complete area is covered, it is recommended to overlap on each side. Water should be used sparingly as the requirement is to cleanse — not to drench. Regardless of the number of hand movements that are needed to satisfy this requirement, all are considered to be part of one complete action.
- While it is obligatory to 'cleanse' the face and hands once, and recommended to do that twice — it is considered inappropriate to do it three or more times, for Imām Ṣādiq عليه السلام prohibited this being done.[1]
- The 'cleansing' that follows immediately after an intention to make *wuḍū'* is considered the 'first'.
- If one intends to perform *wuḍū'* subsequent to having a bath, shower or other wash, it is recommended that such 'cleansing' is done only once after the intention to make *wuḍū'*.
- After 'cleansing' the face, 'cleanse' the right arm and hand from elbow to fingertip, and then the left arm and hand. To ensure that the elbows are

1. We may deduce that this was on the grounds that it would incur unnecessary water usage and encourage people to doubt that they had carried it out properly.

adequately cleansed, it is recommended to start this process a little way above the elbows.

- With moistened right palm, wipe the hair from the centre of the head to the hairline, and the upper part of each foot starting at the toes and ending at the ankle.
- While it is required to moisten any scalp visible through the hair, there is no requirement to moisten any that is not. It is not acceptable, for those with very long hair, to moisten only the tips of their hair — the requirement is to wipe the head.

Ghusl

To have a shower — *ghusl* — sometimes also called 'the greater ablution', is obligatory prior to prayer and other acts of worship in the following circumstances:

Sexual intercourse and the emission of semen — *janābah*.

After semen is discharged, regardless of whether this occurs during sleep or wakefulness, or when penetration occurs during sexual intercourse, if ejaculation occurs or not, a shower becomes necessary to prepare one for any act of worship.

Menstruation — *ḥayḍ*

After the menstrual flow has stopped, a shower becomes necessary to prepare a woman for any act of worship.

Non-menstrual bleeding — *istiḥaḍah*

There are three categories of such occurrence:

1. Slight

Requirement:

To cleanse — change sanitary towel and make *wuḍū'* prior to offering each of the five *ṣalāt*.

2. Heavy

Requirement:

To perform *ghusl* before offering *Fajr ṣalāt*. Cleanse — change sanitary towel and make *wuḍū'* prior to offering *Ḍuḥr*, *ʿAṣr*, *Maghrib* and *ʿIshā' ṣalāt*.

3. Very heavy
Requirement:
To perform *ghusl* before *Fajr*, before *Ḍuḥr* and before *Maghrib ṣalāt*. Cleanse — change sanitary towel and make *wuḍū'* prior to offering *'Aṣr* and *'Ishā' ṣalāt*.

Childbirth — *nifās*
After any bleeding occurs while giving birth — *nifās* — which may be for a few minutes or continue for some ten days, a shower becomes necessary to prepare the mother for any act of worship.

Death — *mawt*
Before burial, the bodies of Muslims are washed three times: once with water in which the leaves of the 'Lote tree' — *sidr* — have been soaked, once with water to which camphor has been added, and once with plain water.[2]

Tayamum
Tayamum is performed in place of *wuḍū'* or bathing the whole body — *ghusl* — in the following six circumstances:

1. When it is not possible to obtain a sufficient quantity of water to perform *wuḍū'* or *ghusl*.

People are required to resolutely seek water for *wuḍū'* and *ghusl* wherever they may happen to be. In populated areas, this means *tayamum* may only be performed when all possibility of finding water has been exhausted. In desert areas, people are required to search for water — on their route and in the surrounding area. In areas of rough terrain or dense forests — where movement may be severely hindered — they should, if conditions permit, search north, south, east and west to a distance of 400 steps — if not, to a distance of at least 200 steps. However, they need not look for water in directions in which they are certain no water is to be found.

2. Prior to the availability of soaps, readily available leaves of the Lote tree were used as a detergent with camphor being employed to preserve the deceased from decay. Despite contemporary soaps and shampoos being equally efficient, in order to follow the *Sunnah* of the Prophet ﷺ, the consensus of jurists is to retain the use of these substances. This has the secondary benefit of helping those who lack funds or live in remote areas.

If there is sufficient time before the next prayer is due — and some certitude that water is to be found a relatively short distance away — they should, if it is not going to be exceedingly difficult, set out to obtain it. However, there is no necessity to set forth on a slim possibility that water may be found. One person may be delegated to bring water for others.

If a person concludes that there is insufficient time to search for water and prays after performing *tayamum* — but later discovers that they would have had ample time — they should repeat the prayer in question.

2. If — due to age, infirmity, danger, extreme difficulty, or lack of receptacle — a person is not able to obtain water, they should perform *tayamum*.

3. People should perform *tayamum* if they have reason to fear that water may endanger their life, or prolong, complicate or aggravate an ophthalmological or other medical condition. However, if warm water for *wuḍū'* and *ghusl* circumvents such danger, it should be used.

4. Those who fear subsequent shortage of drinking water if supplies of water are used for *wuḍū'* and *ghusl* — should perform *tayamum*. This is specifically applicable if consequential shortages are likely to result in humans and animals — for whom one is responsible — suffering intolerable hardship, dehydration or death.

5. If the only water or receptacle available are unsuitable — having been appropriated, for example — *tayamum* should be performed instead of *wuḍū'* and *ghusl*.

6. As it is not appropriate to miss a prayer during its prescribed time — if the performance of *wuḍū'* or *ghusl* would cause this to occur — *tayamum* has to be performed.

The substances that may be used for *tayamum*

Tayamum is performed on clean soil, sand, dried clay or, if necessary, stone.

Requirements of *tayamum*

- The primary requirement is the 'specific intention' to perform *tayamum* — that is, to purify oneself mentally as well as physically in this manner.

- For the palms and fingers of both hands to simultaneously touch or pat the substance being used.

- With the heel of both hands to wipe the entire forehead — from the hair-line to the bridge of the nose.
- Then — in one action — to rub the palm of the left hand over the back — from wrist to fingertip — and to do that also with the palm of the right hand over the back of the left hand.

Direction of the Kaʿbah – qiblah

Qiblah is the Arabic word that denotes the direction of the Kaʿbah — the sacred cube-shaped building in Makkah — towards which all Muslims face when they pray. This action is an exemplification of the Islamic principle, that every human action should be focused upon the single objective of seeking the pleasure of our Almighty Creator. Indeed, facing the direction of the *qiblah* is required for other actions such as circumambulation of the Kaʿbah, burial, the slaughter of beasts and prayers of supplication — *duʿās*. It is also highly recommended that those who recite or read the Qur'ān face in the direction of the *qiblah*.

- While standing or sitting in prayer, the frontal aspect of the body — from head to toe — is aligned to face *qiblah,* the face not being turned away from it. This applies equally to those not able to stand or sit, who should lie, preferably on their right side, but if that too is not possible, on their left side. If neither is possible for them, they should be placed on their back with the soles of their feet aligned to face *qiblah*.
- If a person is required to offer prayer while aboard an aircraft, train or ship they may employ a compass to establish the direction of the *qiblah*. If they do not have a compass available, it is appropriate for them to pray in the approximate direction of the *qiblah*. For example, in North America to face NE, in the United Kingdom to face SE, in Paris, and other European cities on the same latitude, to face E.
- The direction of *qiblah* may be determined by compass, the informed guidance of others, or indicatory niches — *miḥrābs* — of local mosques. However, when no means by which to determine *qiblah* is available, prayer may be offered facing any direction. In spite of this, if time permits, it is recommended that such prayers be offered four times — with the alignment of the body being changed 90° to the right between each prayer.

- If a person believes that the *qiblah* is in one of two directions, they should offer the prayer twice, facing first in the one, and then in the other direction.

Timing for obligatory daily prayer

Within each period of 24 hours it is incumbent on every Muslim to offer five prayers — *ṣalāt* — in their prescribed sequence. Each *ṣalāt* comprises an intention — *niyyat* — and a specific number of cycles of standing upright, bowing with deference and prostration — *rakaʿah* (pl. *rakaʿāt*). It is insufficient simply to go through the motions of prayer. Prayer must inform and motivate all aspects of the believer's existence. It is highly recommended that each prayer be offered at the commencement of the 'preferred time specified in the *aḥadīth*' — *faḍilat al-waqt*.

The time for each prayer is outlined below:

1. *Ẓuhr* — four *rakaʿāt* — at midday.
2. *ʿAṣr* — four *rakaʿāt* — in the late afternoon.
3. *Maghrib* — three *rakaʿāt* — at dusk, as the sky darkens before nightfall.
4. *ʿIshā'* — four *rakaʿāt* — after dusk when full darkness has set.
5. *Fajr* — two *rakaʿāt* — at 'true' dawn — *Fajr al-Ṣadiq*.

For example, if we assume that on a particular day, the time in London for *Ẓuhr* is 12.04 and that sunset is at 4.02:

- The first ten minutes after 12.04 are designated as being the specified time in which to offer *Ẓuhr* — in other words, those ten minutes are exclusively reserved for *Ẓuhr* prayers, and no other prayer may be offered during that time.
- The last ten minutes prior to 4.02 are designated as being the specified time in which to offer *ʿAṣr* — in other words, those ten minutes are exclusively reserved for *ʿAṣr* prayer, and no other prayer may be offered during that time.

However, both *Ẓuhr* and *ʿAṣr* may also be offered at any time between those two specified periods.

In many *aḥadīth,* to pray as early as possible is highly recommended. The Prophet ﷺ once described the reward for a prayer offered at the commencement of each *ṣalāt* time as equivalent to the size of a large camel whilst the reward for prayer offered towards the end of that prayer's time is equivalent to the size of a tiny bird.

Thus, there is a preferred time for each *ṣalāt* to be offered referred to as *faḍilat al-waqt,* explained below:

1. The *faḍilat al-waqt* for the *Ẓuhr* prayer is established in the following manner:
   A rod placed vertically on level ground casts its shadow towards the West as the sun rises. The length of the shadow cast reduces in size as the sun approaches noon and, in places where it is directly overhead, disappears completely. (In Makkah, for example, this occurs on 28th May and 14th July.) The time to start *Ẓuhr* is defined as the moment that the sun passes its highest point and begins to cast its shadow towards the East. The time in which to offer — *faḍilat al-waqt* — the *Ẓuhr* prayer continues until the shadow of the rod reaches four-sevenths of the length of the rod, i.e. just over half its length.

2. The *faḍilat al-waqt* for the *ʿAṣr* prayer starts when the shadow of the rod reaches two-sevenths of the rod's length, and continues till it is equivalent to six-sevenths of the rod's length.

3. The *faḍilat al-waqt* for the *Maghrib* prayer starts when the redness of sunset in the Eastern horizon is at its peak. That is, when the redness of the setting sun has shrunk to cover only the western half of the sky. This *faḍilat* continues until the redness has disappeared completely from the western sky.

4. The *faḍilat al-waqt* for the *ʿIshā'* prayer begins immediately after this, and continues for the first third of the night.

5. The *faḍilat al-waqt* for the *Fajr* prayer is 'true' dawn — *Fajr al-Ṣadiq*. This appears first as a horizontal white thread on the horizon, and then broadens into a 'river of light' of ever increasing clarity and brilliance (... eat and drink until dawn when the whiteness of day becomes distinct from the blackness of night. Qur'ān 2:187). True dawn is not to be

confused with 'first' or 'false' dawn — *Fajr al-Kathib* — that appears as a column of light that increases and diminishes until it finally withers away completely. *Fajr al-Ṣadiq* is technically defined as the instant in the morning when the upper edge of the sun's disc is 18 degrees below the horizon. At certain times of the year, in cities located on 48 degrees of latitude or above, the sun's disc does not descend 18 degrees below the horizon, and for those times, *Fajr al-Ṣadiq* occurs when the upper edge of the sun's disc is 12 degrees below the horizon. This applies in London and similarly located cities between 22 May and 23 July each year.

The details of all these circumstances are explained by Ayatollah Sayyid Fadhel Milani in his *Frequently Asked Questions on Islam,* pages 57–59 (Islam in English Press, London 2001).

- A prayer not offered until after the specified time of its succeeding prayer is considered to be an unfulfilled duty and squandered opportunity. In such circumstance a 'surrogatory prayer' — *qaḍā* — must be offered. In other words, if a person has time to offer only one prayer of four *rakaʿāt* before the specified time for *ʿAṣr* ends, they must offer their *ʿAṣr* prayer, and immediately thereafter their *qaḍā* prayer for *Ẓuhr.*

- In the opinion of all Islamic scholars, a deliberate breach in the sequence in which prayers must be offered renders such prayers invalid.

- If, having made the intention — *niyyat* — and started the *ʿAṣr* prayer, one realizes that *Ẓuhr* has mistakenly been missed, one should instantly transfer one's intention from offering *ʿAṣr* to offering *Ẓuhr*, and continue the prayer as *Ẓuhr*. The *ʿAṣr* prayer must be offered afterwards.

Rulings related to deficiencies during prayer – ṣalāt

- Deliberate major or minor omissions, additions or changes to the obligatory acts of *ṣalāt* render such *ṣalāt* invalid.

- If one comes to realize, during or after *ṣalāt*, that one's *wuḍū'* or *ghusl* is no longer valid, one must abandon that prayer until *wuḍū'* or *ghusl* is again valid. If that prayer's *faḍilat al-waqt* has passed, the prayer should still be offered unless the specified time for the next prayer has come. If that is the case, the surrogatory prayer — *qaḍā* — must be offered.

- If it is realized, during or after *rukūʿ*, that a prostration — *sujud* — of the preceding *rakaʿāt* has been omitted, then that *ṣalāt* is invalid and must be offered correctly. If this is realized prior to *rukūʿ*, *sujud* should immediately be made, followed by all the obligatory actions of *ṣalāt*, from that stage of the prayer onwards. When an error has been corrected during *ṣalāt* it is recommended that two additional *sujuds* be made immediately after that prayer — *Sujud al-Ṣahw* — to correct that oversight.
- If it is realized before the salutation that a *sujud* of the final *rakaʿah* has been omitted, this should be then made and *tashahud* repeated before the salutation.
- If, before the *salām* at the end of the prayer, it is realized that something has been omitted, it should be performed prior to the *salām*.

Conditions to be fulfilled during prayer

Six conditions apply to where prayer may be offered

1. To use a place for prayer it must either be owned, rented, or have the permission of the owner or leaseholder to be used for that purpose. Clearly, mosques and prayer facilities in public places such as universities, hospitals and airports have been provided for people to pray in. One may not knowingly use any thing or place without the legal right to do so.
2. Prayer must be offered in surroundings where it will not be disrupted.
3. There must be sufficient space in which to stand upright, bow and prostrate comfortably.
4. The place must be free of impurities and dry — so that body and clothes are not rendered impure.
5. The point where women place their forehead during prostration should be behind the men. In restricted spaces this may be as far forward as a point just behind the line of the men's knees during prostration.
6. During prostration, the point where the forehead is placed should not be more than the breadth of four fingers above that of the hands, knees and toes.

Islam places great emphasis on *ṣalāt* being offered in mosques. Considered foremost of these are, in the following order:

The Holy Mosque in *Makkah*

The Holy Mosque in *Madinah*

The Holy Mosque in *Kufa*

The Holy Mosque in Jerusalem — *Masjid al-Aqṣā*

These four mosques are followed in preference by the central — *jamiʿ* — mosque of the city, the local mosque and the street market or borough mosque.

Six conditions apply to clothes that are worn during ṣalāt

1. They should not be contaminated by anything that is 'impure in itself' — *Najis al-'Ayn*.
2. They must be permissible for use during prayer, i.e. not stolen or unlawfully obtained.
3. They must not be made of any material from creatures that have not been slaughtered in accordance with Islamic law. Hence leather belts and jackets that may have been made from such materials are removed prior to prayer.
4. They must not be made of material from creatures whose flesh is unlawful to consume, such as carnivores or reptiles.
5. For males — they must not be made of material that includes any silk.
6. For males — they must not be embroidered with gold thread.

Covering of private parts — ʿawrah

- While male pudenda must always remain concealed, this is especially true for *ṣalāt*. It is strongly recommended also to cover the body between navel and knee.

- With the exception of faces and hands, women's bodies and limbs are required to be covered during *ṣalāt*. This clearly requires that clothes should not be, or become, 'see through' in varying lighting conditions.

Acts that invalidate prayer

Prayer is invalidated in twelve circumstances:

1. When realization dawns that an essential requirement of prayer has not been satisfied.
2. When, by accident or intention, *wuḍū'* is invalidated.
3. If, while standing upright, palms are deliberately removed from the thighs in order to fold the arms. Neither the Prophet ﷺ nor the Muslims at the time of the first Caliph folded their arms during *ṣalāt*. This innovation of the second Caliph was prohibited by Imām Ṣādiq عليه السلام when he declared it to be a Magian but not Muslim practice.
4. When *Āmin*' is uttered after *Surat al-Fatiha*. The Prophet ﷺ taught Muslims how to pray and ordered them to 'copy' him. He never uttered *Āmin* after *Surat al-Fatiha* and the only narration that maintains that he ﷺ did so is not regarded as authentic.
5. When a person voluntarily turns away from the *qiblah*.
6. While in prayer it is not legitimate to articulate words or phrases not included in the Qur'ān or used for *dhikr*. If, however, someone greets those in prayer with the words *Salamun Alaikum* — a greeting that demands an obligatory response — it must be done using the phrase *Salamun Alaikum* — words included in the Qur'ān in a variety of places, for example Qur'ān 16:32.
7. When one voluntarily laughs aloud. However, a smile or a small chuckle do not invalidate prayer.
8. The value of any prayer is directly linked to the quality of communication with the Creator. While tears or sobs of fear engendered by Allāh's awesome Omnipotence and Omnipresence do not detract attention from Him, tears shed over the affairs of this world clearly indicate that thoughts and actions are no longer focused on Him — a situation that renders such prayer meaningless.

9. When untoward actions alter the prescribed form of the prayer. The form of prayer is clearly altered if a coat is removed, shirtsleeves rolled up or other such action not associated with prayer. However, small gestures that contribute to reducing a disturbance and promote concentration, for example one to silence a child or indicate that someone who is not praying should answer a knock at the door, are acceptable.

10. When one eats or drinks anything — other than during a recommended *ṣalāt* before *Fajr* — on a day that intention has been made to fast, and the time for fasting is due to commence prior to the prayer ending. In this specific circumstance — providing water is within reach and that all acts that invalidate prayer are avoided — water may be drunk.

11. When continuing doubts are entertained regarding the number of *rakaʿāt* that have been offered during any prayer — because such doubt evidences the absence of concentration.

    Doubts regarding the number of *rakaʿāt* for *Fajr* and *Maghrib* prayers invalidate *ṣalāt*. However, doubts over the number of *rakaʿāt* offered during *Ẓuhr*, *ʿAsr*, and *ʿIshā'* are effaced by the offering of *Ṣalāt al-Iḥtyāṭ* — precautionary prayer — after the prayer has been completed.

12. If deliberate omissions/additions are made to any element of prayer.

Prayer itself

Athān and iqamāh

The history of the *athān*.

Although the *athān* was amongst the very first practices of the Muslim community there are contradictory reports in the *aḥadīth* over how this custom came into being.

- Bukhāri, Muslim, Tirmithi and Nissa'i narrate on the authority of Abdullah ibn ʿUmar that when Muslims in Madinah were gathering for *ṣalāt* they had no means to announce to others that the prayer was about to commence. Some suggested bells, as used in Christian churches, others a ram or ibex horn — *Shofar* — as used by the Jews. But ʿUmar suggested that one member of the congregation call the others to prayer. At this point, the Prophet ﷺ said, 'O Bilal, go and call them to prayer.'

Ṣaḥiḥ Bukhāri, Vol 1, p.306
Ṣaḥiḥ Muslim, Vol 1, p.285
Sunan al-Tirmithi, Vol 1, p.362
Sunan al-Nisaʿi, Vol 2, p.2
Musnad of Aḥmad ibn Ḥanbal, Vol 2, p.148

- Tirmithi and Abu Dāwūd narrate on the authority that Abdullah ibn Zayd told them:

  'I dreamed about a man with a bell just as the Prophet ﷺ was ordering a bell be used to call people to prayer. I asked him, "Will you sell me your bell?" He asked why I wanted it and I replied, "To call people to prayer". He then asked if I would like him to teach me a better way to do this. To my positive response he taught me the *Athān* and *Iqamāh*. In the morning I told the Prophet ﷺ about my dream and he, delighted by it, said that it constituted clear guidance on what to do, and promptly ordered Bilal to undertake that task'. When ʿUmar heard this story he too came to the Prophet ﷺ and said, 'By He who sent the truth with you, I had precisely the same dream as Abdullah ibn Zayd.' The Prophet ﷺ then praised Allāh for such bountiful blessings.

  Sunan al-Tirmithi, Vol. 1, p.358
  Sunan abi Dāwūd, Vol. 1, p.135

- The Imāmiyah and Zaydiyah accept that the first *athān* to be called was during the 'Night Journey' where the Prophet ﷺ learned its detail.

  Al-Ḥalabi reports that Muḥammad ibn al-Ḥanafiyah told him that he was incensed by the nonsense spoken of the *athān* and *iqamāh* being inspired by anyone's dream. It is, he said, 'sheer fantasy that these could be based upon images, of real or imaginary characters, places or events, that happen to pass through the mind of a sleeping person. The *athān* was taught to the Prophet ﷺ during the Night Journey.'

  Al-Sirah al-Ḥalabiyah, Vol. 2, p.300

Numerous authentic *aḥadīth* in the collections of *Al-Kafi*, *Biḥar al-Anwār* and *Wasa'il al-Shi'ah* consistently report that the Prophet ﷺ learned the *athān* and *iqamāh* from Jibrā'īl during the Night Journey.

Prayer comprises:

Intention – Niyyat

The foremost intention and sole motive must be to fulfil obediently a specific injunction of The Creator, and to remain aware of this throughout the prayer. There is no need to enunciate the intention but if the mind drifts and concentration is lost, the prayer is rendered meaningless.

Announcing that prayer has commenced

The words *'Allāhu Akbar'* — *Takbirat al-Iḥram* — must be clearly and accurately pronounced in order to announce that prayer has commenced. This specific requirement must be fulfilled while steadily standing upright. Those who are physically unable to articulate these words must try to fulfil the requirement as best they can.

It is recommended when enunciating the words *'Allāhu Akbar'* — at the commencement of prayer and also when they occur during the prayer — to signify surrender to the will of Allāh Almighty by raising both hands parallel to the ears, with palms facing the *qiblah*.

The three main postures of *ṣalāt* are: Standing upright, Bowing in deference and Prostration in humility. In profound theological discussion each is considered to reflect a different aspect of Islamic Belief in the Oneness of Allāh — There is no Divinity other than Allāh. Standing reflects Unity of Actions, Bowing Unity of Attributes and Prostration Unity of Essence.

Standing upright – qiyam

When Imām Muḥammad Al-Baqir asked his father ʿAli ibn al-Ḥusayn عليه السلام why he turned pale while standing upright in *ṣalāt*, he replied, 'By Allāh, it is because I am conscious of whom I stand before' (*Wasa'il al-Shīʿah*, Vol. 4, p.685). This *ḥadīth* reveals the awesome significance of *qiyam* in submission to the Might and Majesty of Allāh. It is only achieved when the things of this world are completely overshadowed by consciousness of Allāh. While thus aware and while still in this position to recite Qur'ānic *āyat* before going into *rukūʿ*.

Those who are elderly or infirm are exempt from standing and may fulfil this aspect of the prayer while seated. However, if they are able to stand with the aid of a stick or chair they should do so.

Qur'ānic recitation

This comprises the opening *sūrah* plus another short *sūrah* of the Qur'ān — *Qirāah*. The first and second *raka'ah* of every prayer must commence with the recitation of Qur'ān 1:1–7 (*Sūrat al-Fatiḥah* also known as *Sūrat al-Ḥamd*) and be followed by the recitation of any other complete *sūrah*.[3] A few of these are listed.

AL-FATIḤAH — THE OPENER — QUR'ĀN 1

1. In the name of Allāh, the Beneficent, the Most Merciful.
2. Praise Allāh Lord of the Worlds
3. The Most Beneficent, Most Merciful;
4. Master of the Day of Judgement.
5. It is You whom we worship and Your support that we implore.
6. Guide us to the Straight Path,
7. The way of those whom You reward; not the way of those who incite Your wrath or go astray.

Al-Fatiḥah phonetic transliteration — سُورَةُ الفَاتِحَةِ

1. *Bismillahir Raḥmānir Raḥīm* — بِسْمِ اللَّهِ الرَّحْمَٰنِ الرَّحِيمِ ①
2. *Al-Ḥamdu li-Llahi Rabbil Ālamīn* — الْحَمْدُ لِلَّهِ رَبِّ الْعَالَمِينَ ②

3. According to the *aḥadīth* of Ahl al-Bayt, *Sūrah* number 93 known as Al-Ḍuḥā and *Sūrah* number 94 known as Al-Inshiraḥ are regarded, for the purposes of *ṣalāt*, to be a single *sūrah*. This too applies to *Sūrahs* 105 and 106.

3. *Ar-Raḥmān ir-Raḥīm*

ٱلرَّحۡمَٰنِ ٱلرَّحِيمِ ٣

4. *Māliki Yawmid Dīn*

مَٰلِكِ يَوۡمِ ٱلدِّينِ ٤

5. *Iyyaka naʿabudu wa iyyaka nastaʿin*

إِيَّاكَ نَعۡبُدُ وَإِيَّاكَ نَسۡتَعِينُ ٥

6. *Ihdinas ṣiraṭal mustaqīm*

ٱهۡدِنَا ٱلصِّرَٰطَ ٱلۡمُسۡتَقِيمَ ٦

7. *Ṣiraṭal Lathina anʿamta ʿalayhim; Ghairil Maghḍubi ʿalayhim walaḍ ḍālīn*

صِرَٰطَ ٱلَّذِينَ أَنۡعَمۡتَ
عَلَيۡهِمۡ غَيۡرِ ٱلۡمَغۡضُوبِ عَلَيۡهِمۡ
وَلَا ٱلضَّآلِّينَ ٧

AL-TAWḤID — MONOTHEISM — ALSO CALLED AL-IKHLĀṢ — SINCERITY — QUR'ĀN 112

In the name of Allāh, the Beneficent, the most Merciful.

1. Say, 'He, Allāh, is Unique,
2. It is upon Allāh that all depend.
3. He fathers none nor has Himself been fathered.
4. And there are none like Him'.

Al-Tawḥid phonetic transliteration

سُورَةُ الإِخۡلَاصِ

Bismillahir Raḥmānir Raḥīm

بِسۡمِ ٱللَّهِ ٱلرَّحۡمَٰنِ ٱلرَّحِيمِ

1. *Qul huwa Allāhu aḥad*

قُلۡ هُوَ ٱللَّهُ أَحَدٌ ١

2. *Allāhuṣ ṣamad*

ٱللَّهُ ٱلصَّمَدُ ٢

3. *Lam yalid wa lam yulad*

لَمۡ يَلِدۡ وَلَمۡ يُولَدۡ ٣

4. *Wa lam yakun lahu kufwan aḥad*

وَلَمۡ يَكُن لَّهُۥ كُفُوًا أَحَدُۢ ٤

Bowing in deference — rukūʿ

Recitation — *qirat* — is followed by the intention to bow in deference, i.e. bend directly forwards from the waist, to the extent that fingertips rest upon the knees. When the body is steady in that position, to pronounce three times in Arabic, I glorify Allāh — *Subḥana Allāh*. If one prefers, this may be extended to, I glorify my Lord, who is Supremely Glorious and I praise Him — *Subḥana Rabbi al-ʿAẓīm wa bi ḥamdih*.

- *Rukūʿ* should convey absolute faith and submission to the Lord without regard for how He might treat you.
- After completing the above one stands upright and enunciates, Allāh hears those who praise Him — *Samiʿa Allāhu Liman Hamidah*. When steady in that position, intention is made to prostrate oneself in humility and this is immediately thereafter done.
- (Those for whom it is not possible to bend directly forwards from the waist, should indicate their intention with their head. They may find it easier to pray while sitting on a chair.)

Prostration — sujud

Two prostrations — *sajdah* — follow *rukūʿ* in every *ṣalāt*.[4] The intention should be to express utter humility with forehead, palms, knees and big toes touching the earth. When stable in that position to enunciate three times, I glorify Allāh — *Subḥanā Allāh*. If one prefers, this may be extended to, I glorify my Lord the Most High and praise Him — *Subḥana Rabbi al-Aʿla wa bi ḥamdih*.

- This is done because, when 'Glorify your Lord who is Supremely Glorious' was revealed in Qur'ān 56:74, the Prophet ﷺ said, 'Include this in *dhikr* for *rukūʿ*' and when 'Glorify your Lord who is Most High' was revealed in Qur'ān 87:1 the Prophet ﷺ said, 'Include this in the *dhikr* for *sujud*.'
- After the first *sajdah* one sits upon the legs with feet crossed and, when stable in this position, enunciates *Allāhu Akbar* before going into the prostration of the second *sajdah*.

4. The only prayers that do not include either *rukūʿ* or *sujud* are those offered for the dead — *Ṣalat al-Janazah*.

- After the second *sajdah* one stands up for the *qiyam* of a second and identical *raka'ah*.

Offering (the invocation) — qunūt

It is recommended that *qunūt* be recited while standing upright — *qiyam* — just before the *rukū'* of the second *raka'ah* of every *ṣalah*. To do this, open hands are held before the face, fingers together, palms uppermost, and with eyes focused on them the *dhikr* of *qunūt* is enunciated (except for congregational prayers, in which this is done by the Imām). *Qunūt* may consist of any invocation such as, 'O Lord, grant us all that is good in this world and the world to come, and save us from chastisement by fire' — '*Rabbana ātina fid dunya ḥasanah, wa fil Ākherati ḥasanah, wa Qina 'athab an Nāār*' (Qur'ān 2:201).[5]

Bearing witness — tashahud

In the second *raka'ah* of every *ṣalah* as well as in the last *raka'ah* of every *ṣalah* — while sitting on the left thigh with the upper part of the right foot rested on the sole of the left foot and with hands on thighs — one must enunciate:

Phonetic transliteration

Al-ḥamdu li-Llah, ashadu an la ilaha il-allāh waḥdahu la sharika lah

Wa ashadu anna Muḥammadan 'abduhu wa Rasūluh

Allāhuma ṣalli 'ala Muḥammadin wa āli Muḥammad,

Wa taqabbal shafa'atahu warfa' darajatah

Translation

All praise is for Allāh and I testify that there is no Divinity other than Allāh,

the One who is without partner,

And I testify that Muḥammad is His Servant and Messenger,

O Allāh, send Your blessing to Muḥammad and his progeny,

Accept his intercession, and elevate his rank.

5. It is recommended for the *qunūt* of *Salāt al-Witr*, which is one single *raka'ah* of the voluntary midnight prayer, to ask Allāh forgiveness for forty believers.

Ending the prayer — Salām

Once the affirmation — *tashahud* — is completed in the final *rakaʿah* of a prayer, the closing act is to enunciate:

Phonetic transliteration

> *Assalamu ʿalayka ayyuhan Nabi wa raḥmatullahi wa barakatuh*
>
> *Assalamu ʿalayna wa ʿala ʿibadillahi ṣālihin.*
>
> *Assalamu ʿalaykum wa raḥmatullahi wa barakatuh.*

Translation

> O Prophet, Allāh's peace, blessings and grace be upon you,
>
> Also Allāh's peace be on us and upon all pious servants of Allāh.
>
> Allāh's peace and blessings be on you all.

Special circumstances

There are circumstances in which flexibility is appropriate, namely:

Prayer whilst travelling

Prayers of four *rakaʿāt* — cycles of standing upright, bowing and prostration — are shortened to only two *rakaʿāt* during travel, regardless of the purpose of the journey. This ruling is based upon the *āyah*, 'There is no blame on you for shortening your prayers during journeys, if fearful that disbelievers might harry you' (Qur'ān 4:101).

- Muslim reports in his *Ṣaḥiḥ* that ʿUmar asked the Prophet ﷺ the meaning of the phrase, 'there is no blame upon you' and he ﷺ replied, 'This is a concession that Allāh has granted, so accept it and be grateful.' Both Bukhāri and Muslim record that Anas ibn Mālik reported, 'We travelled from Madinah to Makkah with the Prophet ﷺ and throughout the journey he ﷺ only offered two *rakaʿāt* until we returned to Madinah.' This referred specifically to the *Ẓuhr*, *ʿAṣr* and *ʿIshā'* prayers.
- Thus, this concession applies to return journeys of 44 km/28 miles or more, but not to shorter distances.

- A traveller's intention, when setting off, must have been to undertake a return journey of 44 km/28 miles or more.
- The distance of 44 km/28 miles is calculated from one's town of residence regardless of where a journey may have started.
- It goes without saying that the purpose of the journey has to be lawful to benefit from Allāh's concession.
- People whose livelihoods involve long-distance travel do not qualify for this concession.
- The benefit commences immediately after the outer reaches of the town of residence have been passed.

Effects of the prayer being shortened

- Those who start their journey prior to noon — during the month of Ramaḍan or during any other fast — break their fast and shorten their prayers. However, those who start their journeys after midday do not break their fast despite their prayer being shortened.
- Those who travel for six months of the year, or for three days or more each week, do not meet the criteria for prayers to be shortened.
- Travellers who stay the minimum of ten days or more in a town are considered temporary residents and thus do not meet the criteria for prayers to be shortened.

Prayer at the time of solar and lunar eclipse and at times of disasters that are secularly described as 'Acts of God'

There are differences between the events referred to in the items above.

- Solar and lunar eclipses are regular, predictable events observable from a wide variety of places throughout the world; 'Acts of God' are local incidents within specific regions.
- Prayers offered at times of solar or lunar eclipse are obligatory, regardless of people fearing such events or not.

- Prayers after uncontrollable events caused by natural forces, for example earthquakes, hurricanes, tornados or other disaster are only obligatory when the safety of the majority of people in a region is threatened by such an event, or its immediate consequences.

Such prayers were taught by the Prophet Muḥammad ﷺ, whose religious guidance Muslims observe, and have nothing whatever to do with superstitious belief.

How to offer such prayers

These prayers consist of two *rakaʿāt*. In each of them the opening *sūrah* and another short *sūrah* of the Qur'ān is recited five times, followed each time by a *rukūʿ*, prior to the first *sajdah*. The same procedure is repeated in the second *rakaʿah*.

ʿĪd Prayer

All Muslims celebrate two special days each lunar year, namely *ʿĪd al-Fiṭr*, to celebrate the completion of one month of fasting, and *ʿĪd al-Aḍḥā*, to commemorate the sacrifice offered by the Prophet Ibrāhīm ؑ. In the *aḥadīth* related by the error-free Imāms, followers of *Ahl al-Bayt* ؑ are recommended to celebrate also *ʿĪd al-Ghadīr*. This *ʿĪd* commemorates the event at Ghadīr Khum where Imām ʿAlī ؑ was appointed to be the successor to the Prophet ﷺ. A congregational *ʿĪd* prayer is only offered at *Fiṭr* and *Aḍḥā*.

How to offer ʿĪd prayers

The *ʿĪd* prayer consists of two *rakaʿāt*. It is highly recommended that in the first of these, the Imām recite the Opening *sūrah* (*Al-Fatiḥah*) and *Sūrah* 87 (*Al-Aʿla*) — followed by five *qunūts* before the *rukūʿ* of the first *rakaʿah*. And for the second *rakaʿah*, the Opening *sūrah* (*Al-Fatiḥah*) and *Sūrah* 91 (*Al-Shams*) — followed by four *qunūts*.

AL-ʿALĀ — THE MOST HIGH — QUR'ĀN 87

In the name of Allāh, the Beneficent, the most Merciful.

1. Glorify the name of your Lord, Most High,
2. Who creates and gives shape and form [to all of His creation].
3. Who ordains [laws] and provides guidance.
4. Who brings forth pastures [and]
5. Then reduces it to arid brown stubble.
6. We enabled you to read so that you need not forget [what you learned]
7. Except for what Allāh wills [you to forget]. For He [alone] knows what [humanity is able to perceive] and what is concealed [from them],
8. We facilitate progress to your easy task.
9. So persevere in reminding [others of the truth, regardless of] whether such reminders [appear] to be beneficial [or not],
10. For those who fear [Allāh] will draw benefit,
11. And those who are arrogant will reject it.
12. [And in the life to come] will have to endure the great fire,
13. In which they neither live nor die.
14. Prosperity is granted to those who purify themselves,
15. And remember the name of their Lord and worship Him.
16. But you [normally] prefer the life of this world,
17. Despite [the life] to come being superior and more enduring,
18. This has been revealed in earlier scriptures,
19. The scriptures of Ibrāhīm and Mūsa.

	Al–ʿAlā phonetic transliteration	سُورَةُ الأَعْلَى
	Bismillahir Raḥmānir Raḥīm	بِسْمِ ٱللَّهِ ٱلرَّحْمَٰنِ ٱلرَّحِيمِ
1.	*Sabbiḥ isma rabbikal aʿlā*	سَبِّحِ ٱسْمَ رَبِّكَ ٱلْأَعْلَى ١
2.	*Allathi khalaqa fasawwā*	ٱلَّذِى خَلَقَ فَسَوَّىٰ ٢
3.	*Wal lathi qaddara fahadā*	وَٱلَّذِى قَدَّرَ فَهَدَىٰ ٣
4.	*Wal lathi akhrajal marʿā*	وَٱلَّذِىٓ أَخْرَجَ ٱلْمَرْعَىٰ ٤
5.	*Faja ʿalahu ghuthā'an aḥwā*	فَجَعَلَهُۥ غُثَآءً أَحْوَىٰ ٥
6.	*Sanuqri 'uka falā tansā*	سَنُقْرِئُكَ فَلَا تَنسَىٰٓ ٦
7.	*Illa mā shā'a Allāhu innahu yaʿlamul jahara wa mā yakhfā*	إِلَّا مَا شَآءَ ٱللَّهُ ۚ إِنَّهُۥ يَعْلَمُ ٱلْجَهْرَ وَمَا يَخْفَىٰ ٧
8.	*Wa nuyassiruka lil yusrā*	وَنُيَسِّرُكَ لِلْيُسْرَىٰ ٨
9.	*Fathakkir in nafaʿatith thikrā*	فَذَكِّرْ إِن نَّفَعَتِ ٱلذِّكْرَىٰ ٩
10.	*Sayath–thakkaru man yakhshā*	سَيَذَّكَّرُ مَن يَخْشَىٰ ١٠
11.	*Wa yatajannabuhal ashqā*	وَيَتَجَنَّبُهَا ٱلْأَشْقَى ١١
12.	*Allathi yaṣlan nāral kubrā*	ٱلَّذِى يَصْلَى ٱلنَّارَ ٱلْكُبْرَىٰ ١٢
13.	*Thumma lā yamutu fihā wa lā yaḥyā*	ثُمَّ لَا يَمُوتُ فِيهَا وَلَا يَحْيَىٰ ١٣
14.	*Qad aflaḥa man tazakkā*	قَدْ أَفْلَحَ مَن تَزَكَّىٰ ١٤
15.	*Wa thakaraāsma rabbihi faṣalā*	وَذَكَرَ ٱسْمَ رَبِّهِۦ فَصَلَّىٰ ١٥
16.	*Bal tu'thirunal ḥayātad dunyā*	بَلْ تُؤْثِرُونَ ٱلْحَيَوٰةَ ٱلدُّنْيَا ١٦

17. *Wal akhiratu khayrun wa abqā* وَٱلۡأٓخِرَةُ خَيۡرٞ وَأَبۡقَىٰٓ ١٧

18. *Inna hāthā lafiṣ ṣuḥufil ūlā* إِنَّ هَٰذَا لَفِي ٱلصُّحُفِ ٱلۡأُولَىٰ ١٨

19. *Ṣuḥufi Ibrāhima wa Mūsā* صُحُفِ إِبۡرَٰهِيمَ وَمُوسَىٰ ١٩

AL-SHAMS — THE SUN — QUR'ĀN 91

In the name of Allāh, the Beneficent, the most Merciful.

1. Consider the sun and its radiance,
2. And the moon that reflects the sun!
3. Consider the day as it illumines the world,
4. And the night that enshrouds it in darkness!
5. Consider the wonder of the heavens,
6. And the earth in all its expanse!
7. Consider the soul in all its perfection,
8. Equipped with the ability to distinguish between right and wrong.
9. Prosperity is attained by it [the soul] being purified,
10. And failure is the result of it being corrupted.
11. The Thamud [tribe] rejected Truth and rebelled,
12. When their vile member rose to [slay the she camel],
13. Despite Allāh's messenger telling them, 'This is Allāh's creature, let her drink'.
14. They denied the truth of what he said and hamstrung it. As a result, the Lord witnessed their being completely obliterated.
15. It was not He who was to blame for what they [brought upon themselves].

Al–Shams phonetic transliteration	سُورَةُ الشَّمْسِ
Bismillahir Raḥmānir Raḥim	بِسْمِ ٱللَّهِ ٱلرَّحْمَٰنِ ٱلرَّحِيمِ
1. *Wash shamsi wa ḍuḥāha*	وَٱلشَّمْسِ وَضُحَىٰهَا ١
2. *Wal qamari itha talāha*	وَٱلْقَمَرِ إِذَا تَلَىٰهَا ٢
3. *Wan nahāri itha jallāha*	وَٱلنَّهَارِ إِذَا جَلَّىٰهَا ٣
4. *Wal layli itha yaghāshāha*	وَٱلَّيْلِ إِذَا يَغْشَىٰهَا ٤
5. *Was samā'i wamā banāha*	وَٱلسَّمَآءِ وَمَا بَنَىٰهَا ٥
6. *Wal arḍi wamā ṭaḥāha*	وَٱلْأَرْضِ وَمَا طَحَىٰهَا ٦
7. *Wa nafsin wa mā sawwāha*	وَنَفْسٍ وَمَا سَوَّىٰهَا ٧
8. *Fa'alhamahā fujūrahā wa taqwāha*	فَأَلْهَمَهَا فُجُورَهَا وَتَقْوَىٰهَا ٨
9. *Qad aflaḥa man zakkaha*	قَدْ أَفْلَحَ مَن زَكَّىٰهَا ٩
10. *Wa qad khāba man dassāha*	وَقَدْ خَابَ مَن دَسَّىٰهَا ١٠
11. *Kaththabat Thamuudu bi ṭaghwāha*	كَذَّبَتْ ثَمُودُ بِطَغْوَىٰهَآ ١١
12. *Ithin baʿatha ashqāha*	إِذِ ٱنۢبَعَثَ أَشْقَىٰهَا ١٢
13. *Faqāla lahum rasūlul lāhi nāqatal lāhi wa suqyāha*	فَقَالَ لَهُمْ رَسُولُ ٱللَّهِ نَاقَةَ ٱللَّهِ وَسُقْيَٰهَا ١٣
14. *Fakaththabūhu fa ʿaqarūhu fadamdama ʿalayhim rabbuhum bithan bihim fasawwāha*	فَكَذَّبُوهُ فَعَقَرُوهَا فَدَمْدَمَ عَلَيْهِمْ رَبُّهُم بِذَنۢبِهِمْ فَسَوَّىٰهَا ١٤
15. *Wa lā yakhāfu ʿuqbāha*	وَلَا يَخَافُ عُقْبَٰهَا ١٥

Then, a specific *duʿā* is recited during *qunūt* namely:

Translation
O Lord of Grandeur and Might, Lord of Generosity and Omnipotence, Lord of Pardon and Mercy, Lord of Righteousness and Forgiveness, I beseech you on this auspicious day you have made celebratory for the Muslim community, for You to grant Your Mercy and Blessing to the Prophet Muḥammad ﷺ and his progeny and bestow upon me every goodness that You bestowed upon the Prophet Muḥammad ﷺ and his progeny and safeguard me from every misfortune that You safeguarded the Prophet Muḥammad ﷺ and his progeny from. O Allāh, I ask you for the best of what Your most pious and devout servants asked, and seek the same protection that Your most pious and devout servants sought.

Phonetic transliteration
Allāhumma ahl al-Kibriyā' wal ʿAẓamah, wa ahl al-Judi wal Jabarūt wa ahl al-ʿAfwi wal Raḥmah, wa ahl al-Taqwa wal Maghfirah, asa'luka bihaqqi hatha alyawm allathi jaʿaltahu lil Muslimīna ʿIdan wa li-Muḥammadin ﷺ *thukhran wa maizda an tusallia ala Muḥammadin wa āli Muḥammad wa an tudkhilani fi kulli khairin adkhalta fihi Muḥammadan wa āla Muḥammad wa an tukhrejani min kulli sū' akhrajta minhu Muḥammadan wa āla Muḥammad. Allāhumma inni asaluka khaira ma sa'laka minhu ʿibaduka alṣalihūn wa aʿuthu bika mima istaʿatha minhu ʿibaduka* alṣalihūn.

أَللّـهُمَّ أَهْلَ الْكِبْرِياءِ وَالْعَظَمَةِ، وَأَهْلَ الجُودِ وَالجَبَرُوت، وَأَهْلَ الْعَفْوِ وَالرَّحْمَةِ، وَأَهْلَ التَّقْوى وَالمَغْفِرَةِ، أَسْأَلُكَ بِحَقِّ هذَا الْيَومِ الَّذي جَعَلْتَهُ لِلْمُسْلِمينَ عيداً، وَلِمحَمَّدٍ صَلَّى اللهُ عَلَيْهِ وَآلِهِ ذُخْراً وَشَرَفاً وَمَزيْداً، أَنْ تُصَلِّيَ عَلى مُحَمَّدٍ وَآلِ مُحَمَّدٍ، وَأَنْ تُدْخِلَني في كُلِّ خَيْرٍ أَدْخَلْتَ فيهِ مُحَمَّداً وَآلَ مُحَمَّدٍ، وَأَنْ تُخْرِجَني مِنْ كُلِّ سُوءٍ أَخْرَجْتَ مِنْهُ مُحَمَّداً وَآلَ مُحَمَّدٍ صَلَواتُكَ عَلَيْهِ وَعَلَيْهِمْ، أَللّـهُمَّ إِنّي أَسْأَلُكَ خَيْرَ ما سَأَلَكَ مِنْهُ عِبادُكَ الصّالِحُونَ، وَأَعُوذُ بِكَ مِمَّا اسْتَعاذَ مِنْهُ عِبادُكَ الْصّالِحُونَ

After the *ʿĪd* prayer, the Imām delivers two sermons with a short pause in between the first and the second.

- In the first he details the significance of the fast or the pilgrimage and the value of spiritual purification. The second is to emphasize the importance of the Muslim *ummah* remaining united and responsive to the needs of those less fortunate than themselves.
- There is no *athān* or *iqāmah* called for *ʿĪd* prayers. Repetition of the words '*aṣ-ṣalah*' three times suffices. The time for *ʿĪd* prayer is from sunrise to midday and there is no *qaḍā* offered for a missed *ʿĪd* prayer once its time has passed.

Congregational prayers

Muslims are encouraged to offer prayer in congregation and it is considered that the larger the congregation, the greater the blessing of the prayer will be. Authentic *aḥadīth* record that congregational prayer has 25 times greater benefit than prayer not offered in congregation. Indeed, it is not considered appropriate for anyone to abandon congregational prayer without justifiable excuse. Even if one has already offered a specific prayer, it is highly recommended to join a congregation about to offer it. Those who frequently entertain doubts concerning the correctness of their prayers are required to alleviate such doubts by offering their prayers in congregation.

The qualifications required by those who lead congregational prayer

To lead congregational prayer the Imām must be adult, sane, *Ithna Asheri Shiʿah* and *ʿAdil* — righteous. Further, the Imām needs to be well acquainted with rulings that relate to prayers in general and, in particular, those that relate to congregational prayer. A male may lead both genders but a woman may only lead other women. Those not able to stand, bow or prostrate may not lead congregational prayers.

- While the Imām delivers the opening *sūrah* and second short *sūrah* of the Qur'ān — in the first and second *rakaʿāt* — those who follow must remain silent. However, members of the congregation are required to participate in a soft voice, so as not to be overheard — 'sotto-voce' — in the recitation of all the other passages the Imām recites.

- Those who join congregational prayer — prior to the Imām raising his head from *rukūʿ* in the first *rakaʿah* — utter *Takbir al-Iḥrām*, follow the Imām and are considered to have started the prayer together with the congregation. Those who join later than this must wait until the Imām stands for the next *rakaʿah*.

Making up for missed prayers

When any obligatory prayer is missed, whatever the reason, it must be made up for. It is highly recommended for this to be done as soon as is possible. However, if one is not absolutely clear about the precise number of prayers that need to be compensated for, to be on the safe side, one should adopt the maximum that one is certain will fulfil these missed obligations.

- Missed prayers are to be compensated for in the form that they were missed, e.g. those shortened during travel should be offered in shortened form. One has to specify in the *niyyah* that the prayer to be offered is in compensation.

The prayer for the departing soul (Ṣalāt al-Janāzah)

Ṣalāt al-Janāzah should be offered as soon as possible after the deceased's body has been bathed, shrouded and anointed with camphor. The *Ṣalāt al-Janāzah* may take place at home, in a mosque, graveyard or elsewhere in the open. Although women may not enter a mosque during periods of menstruation — *ḥayḍ* — they may enter Islamic centres not designated as mosques. A building is only officially recognized as a mosque after the owner, donor or charity — *waqf* — committee in charge of it, announces the intention for it to be designated as such. Although the state of ritual purity — *wuḍū'* — is a requirement of *ṣalah*, in circumstances in which the making of *wuḍū'* is likely to result in the *Ṣalāt al-Janāzah* being missed, it may be offered even if one is not in the state of *wuḍū'*. This applies equally to women in *ḥayḍ*, absolved from the duties of *ṣalah*, who may join at one side of the congregation.

- This is a manifestation of Allāh's mercy for, no matter what their circumstance, all may participate in prayer for a departed soul. *Ṣalāt al-Janāzah* is the only *ṣalah* for which no *athān* or *iqamāh* is called. The only time both *athān* and *iqamāh* are called and not followed by *ṣalāh*, is after the birth of a baby, when the *athān* is called softly in its right ear and the *iqamāh* in its left.

- Congregational *Ṣalāt al-Janāzah* is offered standing facing the direction of the *qiblah*. The deceased's shrouded body, lying on its back, is laid on a bier or in a coffin, in front of the congregation. It is placed with the head to the right of the congregation and the feet to its left. The Imām positions himself in front of the chest area of a woman and the navel of a man. The congregation stands in lines behind the Imām, makes the intention to offer *Ṣalāt al-Janāzah* for the deceased's soul, raise their hands to their ears to pronounce *Allāhu Akbar* — *takbir* — and follow the Imām in reciting the prayer in a low voice. Those unable to stand may of course sit while doing this.

How to offer Ṣalāt al-Janāzah

According to *Imāmiyah fiqh*, both Imām and congregation pronounce five *takbirs* and between each, the Imām recites either the shorter or the longer passages aloud, with the congregation doing so silently. Imām Jafar as-Sadiq ﵇ said, 'Allāh made five prayers obligatory, and appointed one *takbir* for the deceased in the place of each prayer.' He also referred to the Prophet ﷺ offering five *takbirs* for all the deceased, other than hypocrites, for whom he ﷺ only offered four. However, the four Sunni schools of law only consider four *takbirs* to be necessary.

Ṣalāt al-Janāzah becomes obligatory once a deceased Muslim is six years or over.

1st Takbir

Allāhu Akbar

Then either:

I bear witness that there is no Divinity but Allāh and that Muḥammad is Allāh's Messenger.

Phonetic transliteration

Ashhadu an la ilaha illal lah, wa ashhadu anna Muḥammadan Rasulullah.

or:

I bear witness that there is no Divinity but Allāh the One, who has no associates. And I bear witness that Muḥammad is His Servant and Messenger, sent to convey Truth, and give warnings and good tidings before the Day of Judgement.

Phonetic transliteration
Ashhadu an la ilaha illalahu wahdahu la sharika lah. Wa Ashadu anna Muḥammadan abdahu wa Rasuluh, arsalahu bil haqqi bashiran wa nathiran bayna yaday is saʿah.

2nd Takbir
Allāhu Akbar

Then either:

O Lord! Bestow peace and blessings upon Muḥammad and his progeny.

Phonetic transliteration
Alla humma ṣalli ʿala Muḥammadin wa āli Muḥammad.

or:

O Lord! Bestow peace upon Muḥammad and his progeny and bless Muḥammad and his progeny and send Your Mercy upon Muḥammad and his progeny as the best of Your peace, blessing and mercy was bestowed upon Ibrāhīm and his progeny. You are The Praised and The All-Glorious. Bestow peace upon all the Prophets, Messengers and martyrs.

Phonetic transliteration
Alla humma ṣalli ʿala Muḥammadin wa āli Muḥammad wa barik ʿala Muḥammadin wa āli Muḥammad warḥam Muḥammadan wa āla Muḥammadin ka afzali ma ṣallayta wa barakata wa taraḥamta ʿala Ibrahima wa āli Ibrahima innaka Hamidun Majid wa ṣalli ʿala jamiʿil anbiya' wal mursalin, was-shuhada was-ṣiddiqin wa jamiʿi ʿibadilla his-ṣalihin.

3rd Takbir
Allāhu Akbar

Then either:

O Lord! Forgive all believing men and women.

Phonetic transliteration
Allāh hummaghfir lil mu'minina wal mu'minat.

or:

O Lord! Forgive all believing men and women and all Muslim men and women, alive or dead; join us with them by good deeds. You are the Listener of prayers The All Powerful.

Phonetic transliteration
Allāhumma ghfir lil mu'minina wal mu'minat wal muslimina wal muslimat, alahya'i minhum wal amwat tabiʿ baynana wa baynahum bil khayrati innaka mujibud-daʿwat innak ʿala kulli shay'in Qadir.

4th Takbir
Allāhu Akbar

Then either:

O Lord! Forgive this dead person.

Phonetic transliteration
(For a male) — *Allāhumma ghfir li hazal mayyit.*
(For a female) — *Allāhumma ghfir li hazihil mayyit.*

or:

O Lord, this is Your servant the son/daughter of Your servants, Your guest and You are the best of Hosts. O Lord, we know him/her by his/her good conduct but You know him/her better than we do. O Lord, if he/she was a doer of good, increase their good for them. If on the other hand he/she was a doer of evil, forgive him/her. O Lord, lift him/her to the highest level and console the bereaved. You are the All Merciful.

Phonetic transliteration

(For a male) — *Alla humma inna haza ʿabduka wabnu ʿabdika wabnu amatika nazala bika wa anta khayru manzulin bihi Alla humma inna la naʿlamu minhu illa khayra wa anta aʿalamu bihi minna. Alla humma in kana mohsinan fa zid fi ihsanihi wa in kana musi'an fatajawaz anhu waghfir lahu. Allāhumma jʿalhu ʿindaka fi aʿla ʿilliyyin wakhluf ʿala ahlihi fil ghabirin warhamhu bi-rahmatika ya ar hamar Rahimin.*

(For a female) — *Alla humma inna hazihi amatuka wabnatu ʿabdika wabnatu amatika nazalalat bika wa anta khayra manzulin bihi Allāhumma inna la naʿlamu minha illa khayra wa anta aʿalamu biha minna. Allāhumma in kanat mohsinatan fa zid fi ihsaniha wa in kanat musi'atan fatajawaz ʿanha waghfir laha. Allāhumma jʿal ha ʿindaka fi aʿla ʿilliyyin wakhluf ʿala ahliha fil ghabirin warhamha bi-rahmatika ya ar hamar Rahimin.*

5th Takbir

Allāhu Akbar

Voluntary prayers

In section 9.5 we discussed the obligatory — *farḍ* — prayers that constitute a 'pillar' of the Islamic religion. However, as constant communication with the Creator is highly recommended, additional prayers, over and above the obligatory, are commonly offered. Some additional prayers — *nāfilah* (pl. *nawāfil)* — are customarily appended to *farḍ* prayers, others are not.

Voluntary *rakaʿāt* are invariably offered in pairs, i.e. four *rakaʿāt* being made up of two sets of two *rakaʿāt*.

Voluntary prayers that are appended are:

- Two *rakaʿāt* prior to the *Fajr* prayer
- Eight *rakaʿāt* prior to the *Ẓuhr* prayer
- Eight *rakaʿāt* prior to the *ʿAṣr* prayer
- Four *rakaʿāt* after the *Maghrib* prayer

- Two *rakaʿāt* after the *ʿIshā'* prayer while sitting — despite this being considered to equate to only a single *rakaʿah* performed while standing.
- Eleven *rakaʿāt* for the midnight prayer

A total of 34 *rakaʿāt*

Thus, the *rakaʿāt* offered in any one day — 17 *farḍ* + 34 *nawāfil:* total 51.

Voluntary prayers include the following.

The prayer related to Jafar, son of Abu Ṭālib

Numerous authentic reports refer to its outstanding effectiveness as an expression of contrition in seeking forgiveness for major sin. The most appropriate time to offer this four-*rakaʿāt* prayer is thought to be a half hour after sunrise on a Friday morning.

The first pair: In the first *rakaʿah*, *Sūrah* 99 — *Al-Zilzāl* — is recited after *Al-Fatiḥah*, and in the second *rakaʿah*, *Sūrah* 100 — *Al-ʿAdiyāt* — is recited after *Al-Fatiḥah*.

AL-ZILZĀL — THE EARTHQUAKE — QUR'ĀN 99

In the name of Allāh, the Beneficent, the most Merciful.

1. When the earth rocks with dramatic quakes
2. And discharges its burdens
3. And humanity wonders what is happening
4. On that day, all its secrets will be exposed
5. As inspired by your Lord
6. On that day, people will leave [their graves] and assemble in groups to view their deeds
7. Whoever has done an atom's weight of good shall see it
8. And whoever has done an atom's weight of evil shall see it.

Al-Zilzāl phonetic transliteration	سُورَةُ الزَّلْزَلَةِ
Bismillahir Raḥmānir Raḥim	بِسْمِ اللَّهِ الرَّحْمَٰنِ الرَّحِيمِ
1. *Itha zulzilat al arḍu zilzālaha*	إِذَا زُلْزِلَتِ الْأَرْضُ زِلْزَالَهَا ١
2. *Wa Akhrajat al arḍu athqāaha*	وَأَخْرَجَتِ الْأَرْضُ أَثْقَالَهَا
3. *Wa qāal insānu ma lahā*	وَقَالَ الْإِنسَانُ مَا لَهَا ٣
4. *Yawma ithin tuḥadithu akhbāraha*	يَوْمَئِذٍ تُحَدِّثُ أَخْبَارَهَا ٤
5. *Bi anna Rabbaka awḥā lahā*	بِأَنَّ رَبَّكَ أَوْحَىٰ لَهَا ٥
6. *Yawma ithin yaṣduru annāsu ashtātan* *li yuraw aʿmālahum*	يَوْمَئِذٍ يَصْدُرُ النَّاسُ أَشْتَاتًا لِّيُرَوْا أَعْمَالَهُمْ ٦
7. *Faman yaʿmal mithqala tharratin khairan yarah*	فَمَن يَعْمَلْ مِثْقَالَ ذَرَّةٍ خَيْرًا يَرَهُ ٧
8. *Waman yaʿmal mithqala tharratin sharran yarah*	وَمَن يَعْمَلْ مِثْقَالَ ذَرَّةٍ شَرًّا يَرَهُ ٨

AL-ʿADIYĀT — THE CHARGERS — QUR'ĀN 100

In the name of Allāh, the Beneficent, the most Merciful.

1. By the snorting chargers,
2. By the sparks from their striking hooves
3. By those who invade at dawn
4. Generating clouds of dust
5. Penetrating deep [into the enemy's camp]
6. Truly, humans are ungrateful to their Lord
7. And they themselves are witness to this

8. Truly, humanity is devoted to wealth
9. Do they not know that what has been buried will again be brought forth?
10. And that which is in their breasts will be divulged?
11. Truly, their Lord will be aware of their deeds on that day.

Al–ʿAdiyāt phonetic transliteration	سُورَةُ العَادِيَاتِ
Bismillahir Raḥmānir Raḥim	بِسْمِ اللَّهِ الرَّحْمَٰنِ الرَّحِيمِ
1. *Wal ʿAdiyāti ḍabḥā*	وَالْعَادِيَاتِ ضَبْحًا ١
2. *Fal muryati qadḥā*	فَالْمُورِيَاتِ قَدْحًا ٢
3. *Fal mughrirati ṣubḥā*	فَالْمُغِيرَاتِ صُبْحًا ٣
4. *Fa atharna bihi naqʿā*	فَأَثَرْنَ بِهِ نَقْعًا ٤
5. *Fa wasaṭna bihi jamʿā*	فَوَسَطْنَ بِهِ جَمْعًا ٥
6. *Innal insāna li rabbihi lakanūd*	إِنَّ الْإِنسَانَ لِرَبِّهِ لَكَنُودٌ ٦
7. *Wa innahu ʿalā thalika lashahīd*	وَإِنَّهُ عَلَىٰ ذَٰلِكَ لَشَهِيدٌ ٧
8. *Wa innahu li ḥubbil khayri lashadīd*	وَإِنَّهُ لِحُبِّ الْخَيْرِ لَشَدِيدٌ ٨
9. *Afala yaʿlamu itha boʿthira ma fil qubūr*	۞ أَفَلَا يَعْلَمُ إِذَا بُعْثِرَ مَا فِي الْقُبُورِ ٩
10. *Wa ḥuṣṣila ma fiṣ ṣudūr*	وَحُصِّلَ مَا فِي الصُّدُورِ ١٠
11. *Inna Rabbahum bihim yawmaithin lakhabīr*	إِنَّ رَبَّهُم بِهِمْ يَوْمَئِذٍ لَّخَبِيرٌ ١١

The second pair: In the first *raka'ah, Sūrah* 110 — *Al-Naṣr* — is recited after *Al-Fatiḥah* and in the second *raka'ah, Sūrah* 112 — *Al-Ikhlaṣ* — is recited after *Al-Fatiḥah.*

AL-NAṢR — VICTORY — QUR'ĀN 110

In the name of Allāh, the Beneficent, the most Merciful.

1. When Allāh's help and victory come
2. And you see crowds of people accepting Allāh's religion,
3. Then glorify your Lord and ask His forgiveness, for He is truly forgiving.

Al-Naṣr phonetic transliteration	سُورَةُ النَّصْرِ
Bismillahir Raḥmānir Raḥīm	بِسْمِ ٱللَّهِ ٱلرَّحْمَٰنِ ٱلرَّحِيمِ
1. *Itha jāa naṣrul Allāhi wal fatḥ*	إِذَا جَآءَ نَصْرُ ٱللَّهِ وَٱلْفَتْحُ ١
2. *Wa raaytan nāsa* *yadkhuluna fi dinil Lāhi afwaja*	وَرَأَيْتَ ٱلنَّاسَ يَدْخُلُونَ فِي دِينِ ٱللَّهِ أَفْوَاجًا ٢
3. *Fa sabbiḥ bi ḥamdi Rabbika* *was taghfirhu innahu kana tawwaba*	فَسَبِّحْ بِحَمْدِ رَبِّكَ وَٱسْتَغْفِرْهُ إِنَّهُۥ كَانَ تَوَّابًۢا ٣

AL-TAWḤĪD — MONOTHEISM — ALSO CALLED AL-IKHLĀṢ — SINCERITY — QUR'ĀN 112

In the name of Allāh, the Beneficent, the most Merciful.

1. Say, 'He, Allāh, is Unique,
2. It is upon Allāh that all depend.
3. He fathers none nor has Himself been fathered.
4. And there are none like Him'.

Al-Tawḥīd phonetic transliteration	سُورَةُ الإِخْلَاص
Bismillahir Raḥmānir Raḥīm	بِسْمِ ٱللَّهِ ٱلرَّحْمَٰنِ ٱلرَّحِيمِ
1. *Qul huwa Allāhu aḥad*	قُلْ هُوَ ٱللَّهُ أَحَدٌ ١
2. *Allāhuṣ ṣamad*	ٱللَّهُ ٱلصَّمَدُ ٢
3. *Lam yalid wa lam yulad*	لَمْ يَلِدْ وَلَمْ يُولَدْ ٣
4. *Wa lam yakun lahu kufwan aḥad*	وَلَمْ يَكُن لَّهُۥ كُفُوًا أَحَدٌۢ ٤

In both pairs of *raka'āt* the following is repeated — as outlined below:

Translation
Allāh is glorified and praised, there is no Divinity but Him, He is The Most Great.

Phonetic transliteration
'Subḥana Allāhi wal Ḥamdu lilahi wa La ilaha illa Alahu wa Allāhu Akbar'.

15 times after recitation of the two *sūrahs*,

10 times during each *rukū'*,

10 times while standing after *rukū'*,

10 times during each *sajdah*,

10 times while sitting between the two *sajdahs*,

and,

10 times while sitting after the second *sajdah*.

The above glorification — *tasbiḥ* — is thus recited 75 times in each *raka'āh* — taking the total number in this prayer to 300.

- Shaykh Koleini reports, on the authority of Imām Jafar as-Sadiq ﷺ, that he taught one of his companions to recite the following supplication in the last *sajdah* of the fourth *raka'ah*, immediately after the completion of the ten *tasbiḥ*.

Translation

Glorified is the One of Honour and Dignity, Glorified is the Sole source of every bounty, Glorified is the One to whom glorification exclusively belongs, Glorified is the Omniscient One who encompasses all, Glorified is the Sole source of Power and Generosity. O Allāh, I ask by the elements of Glory that uphold Your Throne, by Your abundant Mercy and Your Greatest Name to bestow Your Mercy and Blessing upon Muḥammad ﷺ and his progeny and grant me . . . [mention your individual wishes].

Phonetic transliteration

Subḥana man labisa al'izza wal waqār, Subḥana man ta'aṭafa bil majdi wa takarama bih, Subḥana man la yanbaghi al tasbiḥu illa lah, Subḥana man aḥṣā kulla shayin 'ilmuh, Subḥana thil manni wal niy'am, Subḥana thil qudrati wal karam. Allāhuma ini asaluka bi ma'aqid el'izz min 'arshika wa muntahą al raḥmati min kitabika, wa ismikal 'aẓam wa kalimatik al tāmmah al-lati tamat ṣidqan wa 'adlan salli 'alā Muḥammadin wa ahli baytihi waf'al bi . . .

صلاة جعفر الطيار عليه السلام

سُبْحانَ مَنْ لَبِسَ الْعِزَّ وَالْوَقارَ، سُبْحانَ مَنْ تَعَطَّفَ بِالمجْدِ وَتَكَرَّمَ بِهِ، سُبْحانَ مَنْ لا يَنْبَغِي التَّسْبيحُ إلاّ لَهُ، سُبْحانَ مَنْ أَحْصى كُلِّ شَيْءٍ عِلْمُهُ، سُبْحانَ ذِي المَنِّ وَالنِّعَمِ، سُبْحانَ ذِي الْقُدْرَةِ وَالْكَرَمِ. اَللّـهُمَّ إنّي أَسْأَلُكَ بِمَعاقِدِ الْعِزِّ مِنْ عَرْشِكَ، وَمُنْتَهَى الرَّحْمَةَ مِنْ كِتابِكَ، وَاسْمِكَ الأعْظَمِ، وَكَلِماتِكَ التّامَّةِ الَّتى تَمَّتْ صِدْقاً وَعَدْلاً، صَلِّ عَلى مُحَمَّدٍ وَاَهْلِ بَيْتِهِ وَافْعَلْ بى....

It is considered to be particularly meritorious to recite the above prayer in the Holy Shrine of Imām Riḍa (as). Alamah Majlisi quotes from Shaykh Husayn ibn Abdul Ṣamad through his teachers that, if a visitor to the shrine of Imām Riḍa (as) or other Imāms (as) recites the above prayer, there will be recorded for him many great rewards.
Mafitih-ul-Jinan, Keys of Heavens, translated by Murtaza Lakha, p. 520

The prayer for protection offered after Jumuʿah or Ẓuhr on a Friday

Shaykh Ṭusi reported from Imām Ṣādiq (as), that if a person recites two *rakaʿāt* on a Friday, after *Ẓuhr*, and in each, after *Al-Fatiḥah* recites *Sūrah* 112 — *Al-Ikhlas* — seven times, followed by the supplication below, protection from all afflictions is granted for the coming week, and that Allāh will ensure they remain in the company of Muḥammad ﷺ and Ibrāhīm (as).

Translation
O Allāh please place me in paradise that overflows with Your mercy and in the company of our Prophet Muḥammad ﷺ and his forefather Ibrāhīm (as).

Phonetic transliteration
Allāhuma ijʿalni min ahl al jannah al lati ḥashwuhā al-barakah wa ʿummaruhā al-malaikah maʿa nabiyna Muḥammadin ﷺ *wa abina Ibrahim* (as)

أعمال يوم الجمعة

أَللّـهُمَّ اجْعَلْني مِنْ اَهْلِ الجَنَّةِ الَّتي حَشْوُهَا الْبَرَكَةُ وَعُمّارُهَا المَلائِكَةُ مَعَ
نَبِيِّنا مُحَمَّدٍ صَلَّى اللهُ عَلَيْهِ وَآلِهِ وَأَبينا إِبراهيمَ عليه السلام

Prayer offered to implore the Lord for rain

Although people do not need such prayers in those parts of the world in which there is seldom any shortage of water, many areas do suffer water shortage and drought.

The Prophet ﷺ taught us how we may implore the Lord for rainfall and recommended that several acts be associated with this two-*rakaʿāt* prayer that is followed by an address.

- It is offered in the outskirts of cities, except in Makkah, where it is offered in *Masjid Al-Ḥarām*.
- According to a *ḥadīth* reported from Imām Ṣādiq ؑ, it is better if Muslims fast for three days and offer this prayer on the third.
- When he offered this prayer, the Prophet ﷺ put his cloak on 'inside-out', so that its right shoulder rested upon his left shoulder and vice-versa. When asked why this was so he ﷺ said that it was to symbolize drought being overcome by abundance.
- It is recommended that the Imām face the *qiblah* and repeat *'Allāhu Akbar'* 100 times, that he then turn his head to the right and repeat '*Subḥana Allāh*' 100 times and then to the left, to repeat *'La ilaha illal Allāh'* 100 times prior to facing the congregation and repeating the phrase *'Al Ḥamdu lilahi'* 100 times.

Thereafter, the Imām leads the prayer and delivers his address.

History records that during a time of severe drought, Imām ʿAlī ؑ left the city in order to offer this prayer and deliver the following sermon:

> Be aware, the earth that bears you and the sky that covers you are obedient to their Sustainer (Allāh). They do not bestow their blessing out of pity for you or for any good from you, but do so because that is what they have been commanded to do and they merely obey that command.

Allāh tries His creatures with regard to their evil deeds by decreasing fruits, holding back blessings and sealing treasures, so that those who wish to repent may, and those who were negligent may develop awareness. Allāh Almighty has made the seeking of His forgiveness a means for pouring livelihoods and mercy upon people, 'Seek the forgiveness of your Lord, truly He is the Oft-forgiving, He will send down upon you clouds of abundant rainfall and will provide help for your wealth and offspring' (Qur'ān 71:10–12). 'May Allāh shower mercy upon those who repent and forsake sin. O Allāh, we come from the shelters we have built while our children and beasts cry out for Your mercy, hope for the generosity of Your bounty and remain in fear of

Your chastisement and retribution. Oh Allāh, let us drink from your rainfall, do not forsake us and let the drought take our lives, do not punish us for what the foolish amongst us have committed.'[6]

> Oh Allāh, we have come to complain about something that is not hidden from You. Severe troubles have forced us, famine has driven us, distress and need have reduced us to helplessness. Oh Allāh, we beseech You not to send us back disappointed, not to make us return with downcast eyes and not to treat us according to our own deeds.
>
> Oh Allāh, please pour Your mercy, blessing and sustenance down upon us and let us enjoy rain: to quench our thirst; to produce green herbage and bring to life again that which has withered; to bring about the benefits of freshness, plenitude and ripened fruits. With rain our rivers may flow again, our fields will be irrigated, our plants will regain foliage and the price of food will plummet. You certainly have power over whatever You will.
>
> **Nahj al-Balāghah, Sermon 143**

Prayer offered during each of the first ten days of Dhul-Hijjah

Once in a lifetime pilgrimage to Makkah is obligatory for those who can afford it. However, those unable to go, and those who have already been but nevertheless yearn for the merits of pilgrimage, are recommended to offer two *rakaʿāt* – between the *Maghrib* and *ʿIshā'* prayers — during the first ten nights of Dhul-Hijjah. In both *rakaʿāt*, after reading *Sūrah Al-Fatiḥah* and *Sūrah Al-Ikhlas* the following *āyah* is recited:

> We called Mūsa into Our presence for 30 nights and kept him with Us a further 10 after that to make his stay total 40 nights. Mūsa said to his brother Hārūn, 'Take my place among my people, act appropriately and be cautious not to let mischief-makers influence you.'
>
> **Qur'ān 7:142**

6. This is in reference to Qur'an 7:155 in which the Prophet Mūsa ﷺ selected 70 men of his people to be appointed by the Lord, who in their supplication said, 'Will you destroy us for what the foolish amongst us have done?'

Phonetic transliteration
Bismillahir Raḥmnir Raḥīm
Wa wāʿandā Mūsa thalathina laylatan wa atmamnahā bi ʿashrin, fatamma miqatu Rabbihi arbaʿeena laylah. Wa qāla Mūsa li akhihi Haruna khlufni fi qawmi wa aṣliḥ wa la tattabiʿ sabilal mufsidīn.

Prayers offered during the nights of the Holy Month of Ramaḍan

It is highly recommended to combine the fast of Ramaḍan with nightly prayer. According to authentic *aḥadīth* one should offer 1,000 voluntary *rakaʿāt* over this month in the following manner:

> Over the first 20 days offer 20 *rakaʿāt* each night — eight after *Maghrib* and 12 after *ʿIshā'*.
>
> Over the last ten days, offer 30 *rakaʿāt* each night — 12 after *Maghrib* and 18 after *ʿIshā'*.
>
> On the 19th, 21st, and 23rd offer 100 *rakaʿāt* each night.

Important note

The Prophet ﷺ only stipulated that 'obligatory' prayers be offered in congregation. The custom that was followed during his ﷺ lifetime was for the voluntary prayers of the nights of Ramaḍan to be offered alone by each individual — not in congregation. This practice was continued during Abu Bakr's period in office and, for the first year of his caliphate, ʿUmar fasted over Ramaḍan and offered his prayers in the same manner as the Prophet ﷺ and Abu Bakr had done before him.

However, in the 14th year of the Hijra, ʿUmar and some of his companions entered the mosque in Madinah while those present were offering voluntary prayer — some bowing, some in prostration, some standing and others sitting. He felt displeased by the apparent disorder and was moved to stipulate that all those present offer voluntary prayers in congregation. He further demanded that this be done in all the mosques throughout his dominion. Such congregational prayers came to be known as *Tarāwīḥ*.

However, the error-free Imāms of *Ahl al-Bayt* عليهم السلام continue to follow the *Sunnah* of the Prophet ﷺ and decline this, and all other innovation.

Prayer of greeting offered after entering any mosque

It is recommended to offer two *rakaʿāt* each time one enters a mosque but there are no references to any particular *surahs* being recited. Abu Ḍar reports that he entered the mosque while the Prophet ﷺ was there and he said,

> 'O Abu Ḍar, there is a greeting to be offered to the mosque'; when I asked him ﷺ what that was he ﷺ replied, 'To offer two *rakaʿāt*.'
> **Wasa'il al Shiʿah, Vol. 5, p.248**

Prayer offered on the first night after a burial (Ṣalāt al-Waḥshah)

On the first night after burial, fellow Muslims are recommended to offer two *rakaʿāt* to comfort the soul of the deceased in its new surroundings.

> **The first** *rakaʿah*: *āyat* 2:255–7 — *Al-Kursi* — is recited after *Al-Fatiḥah*.

> **The second** *rakaʿah*: *Sūrah* 97 — *Al-Qadr* — is recited 10 times after *Al-Fatiḥah*.

After this, the request is made, 'O Lord, please bless the Prophet Muḥammad ﷺ and his progeny عليهم السلام and refer the benefit of this prayer to the grave of 'so and so' [the name of the deceased and her/his father].

AL-BAQARAH — THE COW — QUR'ĀN 2

The frequently recited *āyat* — 255–257 — are jointly referred to as:
'Throne Āyat' — '*Ayat ul-Kursi*'.

Translation
In the name of Allāh, the Beneficent, the most Merciful.

255. Allāh! There is no Divinity other than He who is The Living, The Self-Subsisting, The Eternal.[7] He neither tires nor sleeps. It is He who creates all

7. For elaboration on these Divine names refer to *The Source of Islamic Spirituality*, Islam in English Press, 2004, pp. 175–250.

the things in the heavens and on the earth. Who is there who may intercede with Him without His permission? It is He who knows all that is apparent to His creatures, in addition to all that is hidden from them. Without His willing it, none may acquire any of His knowledge. His Throne [Overall Control] encompasses heaven and earth, and He is not fatigued in maintaining them, for He is The Most High, The Supreme [in glory].

256. There can be no coercion regarding matters of faith. Truth has been made clearly distinct from error, hence those who have faith in Allāh and avoid what is false, have indeed clasped the hand of unfailing support that is never abandoned. And Allāh is All Hearing, All Knowing.

257. Allāh is the Guardian of those who believe. It is He who brings them out of darkness into the light. Those who disbelieve and place their faith in things not Divine place reliance on that which takes them from light into darkness and become destined to abide in the fire.

Āyat ul-Kursī phonetic transliteration

Bismillahir Raḥmānir Raḥim

بِسۡمِ ٱللَّهِ ٱلرَّحۡمَٰنِ ٱلرَّحِيمِ

255. *Allāhu la ilaha illa huwal Ḥayul Qayyum. La ta'khuthuhu sinatun wa la nawm. Lahu ma fis samwāti wa ma fil arḍ. Man thal lathi yashfaʿu indahū illa bi ithnihi yaʿlamu ma bayna aydihim wa ma khalfahum, wa la yuḥiṭūna bi shay'in min ʿilmihi illa bima shā'a wasiʿa kursyuhu alāsamāwāti wal arḍa wa la ya'uduhū hifḍuhuma wa huwal aliyul aẓīm.*

ٱللَّهُ لَآ إِلَٰهَ إِلَّا هُوَ
ٱلۡحَيُّ ٱلۡقَيُّومُۚ لَا تَأۡخُذُهُۥ سِنَةٞ وَلَا نَوۡمٞۚ لَّهُۥ مَا فِي ٱلسَّمَٰوَٰتِ وَمَا
فِي ٱلۡأَرۡضِۗ مَن ذَا ٱلَّذِي يَشۡفَعُ عِندَهُۥٓ إِلَّا بِإِذۡنِهِۦۚ يَعۡلَمُ مَا بَيۡنَ
أَيۡدِيهِمۡ وَمَا خَلۡفَهُمۡۖ وَلَا يُحِيطُونَ بِشَيۡءٖ مِّنۡ عِلۡمِهِۦٓ إِلَّا بِمَا
شَآءَۚ وَسِعَ كُرۡسِيُّهُ ٱلسَّمَٰوَٰتِ وَٱلۡأَرۡضَۖ وَلَا يَـُٔودُهُۥ حِفۡظُهُمَاۚ
وَهُوَ ٱلۡعَلِيُّ ٱلۡعَظِيمُ ٢٥٥

256. *La ikraha fid dīni qad tabayanal rushdu min alāghayy, fa man yakfur bil taghuti wa yu'min bil lāhi faqad istamsaka bil ʿurwatil wuthqāla infiṣama laha, wal lahu samiʿun ʿalīm.*

لَآ إِكۡرَاهَ فِي ٱلدِّينِۖ قَد تَّبَيَّنَ ٱلرُّشۡدُ
مِنَ ٱلۡغَيِّۚ فَمَن يَكۡفُرۡ بِٱلطَّٰغُوتِ وَيُؤۡمِنۢ بِٱللَّهِ فَقَدِ
ٱسۡتَمۡسَكَ بِٱلۡعُرۡوَةِ ٱلۡوُثۡقَىٰ لَا ٱنفِصَامَ لَهَاۗ وَٱللَّهُ سَمِيعٌ عَلِيمٌ ٢٥٦

257. *Allāhu waliyul lathina āmanū yukhrijuhum min alāẓulumāti ilal nūr, wal lathina kafaru awliya'uhum alātaghutu yukhrijunahum minal nūri ilal ẓulumāti 'ulaika aṣḥabul nāri hum fiha Khalidūn.*

ٱللَّهُ وَلِيُّ ٱلَّذِينَ ءَامَنُوا۟ يُخْرِجُهُم مِّنَ ٱلظُّلُمَـٰتِ إِلَى ٱلنُّورِ ۖ
وَٱلَّذِينَ كَفَرُوٓا۟ أَوْلِيَآؤُهُمُ ٱلطَّـٰغُوتُ يُخْرِجُونَهُم مِّنَ
ٱلنُّورِ إِلَى ٱلظُّلُمَـٰتِ ۗ أُو۟لَـٰٓئِكَ أَصْحَـٰبُ ٱلنَّارِ ۖ هُمْ فِيهَا
خَـٰلِدُونَ ٢٥٧

AL-QADR — MEASURE — QUR'ĀN 97

In the name of Allāh, the Beneficent, the most Merciful.

1. We revealed this [Divine Writ] on the Night of Measure,
2. And how may you comprehend the Night of Measure?
3. For the Night of Measure is better than a thousand months,
4. During this night, by Allāh's permission, Angels, and the Spirit, bring down details of every matter,
5. And peace reigns till the break of dawn.

Al-Qadr, phonetic transliteration

سُورَةُ ٱلْقَدْرِ

Bismillahir Raḥmānir Raḥim

بِسْمِ ٱللَّهِ ٱلرَّحْمَـٰنِ ٱلرَّحِيمِ

1. *Innā anzalnahu fi laylatil qadr*

إِنَّآ أَنزَلْنَـٰهُ فِى لَيْلَةِ ٱلْقَدْرِ ١

2. *Wa ma adrāka ma laylatul qadr,*

وَمَآ أَدْرَىٰكَ مَا لَيْلَةُ ٱلْقَدْرِ ٢

3. *Laylatul qadri khayrun min alfi shahr*

لَيْلَةُ ٱلْقَدْرِ خَيْرٌ مِّنْ أَلْفِ شَهْرٍ ٣

4. *Tanazzalul malaikatu war ruḥu*
fiha bi ithni rabihim min kuli amr

تَنَزَّلُ ٱلْمَلَـٰٓئِكَةُ وَٱلرُّوحُ
فِيهَا بِإِذْنِ رَبِّهِم مِّن كُلِّ أَمْرٍ ٤

5. *Salamun hiya ḥatta maṭlaʿ il fajr.*

سَلَـٰمٌ هِىَ حَتَّىٰ مَطْلَعِ ٱلْفَجْرِ ٥

Prayer of ghufailah

The name *ghufailah* is derived from the Arabic word for heedlessness — *ghaflah* — which implies that most people are not aware of its merits.

It comprises two *raka'āt* offered between the *Maghrib* and *'Ishā'* prayers. In the first *raka'ah* after *al-Fatiḥah*: the *āyat* 21:87—88 are recited. It is evident that the recitation of these *āyat* is to relieve believers of their woes.[8]

AL-ANBIYĀ — THE PROPHETS — QUR'ĀN 21

In the name of Allāh, the Beneficent, the most Merciful.

87. Remember, Yunus left in anger with no thought of Our being strict with him but later cried from the darkness, 'There is no Divinity other than You. Glory be to You. Truly I was unjust.'

88. Then We responded and comforted him – thus do We relieve those who truly believe.

Al- Anbiyā phonetic transliteration

Bismillahir Raḥmānir Raḥīm

بِسۡمِ ٱللَّهِ ٱلرَّحۡمَٰنِ ٱلرَّحِيمِ

87. *Wa thanūni ith thahaba mughaḍiban faḍanna an lan naqdira alayh, fanādā fiẓ ẓolumati an la ilaha illa ant, subḥanaka inni kuntu min al ẓalimīn.*

وَذَا ٱلنُّونِ إِذ ذَّهَبَ مُغَٰضِبًا فَظَنَّ أَن لَّن نَّقۡدِرَ عَلَيۡهِ
فَنَادَىٰ فِي ٱلظُّلُمَٰتِ أَن لَّآ إِلَٰهَ إِلَّآ أَنتَ سُبۡحَٰنَكَ إِنِّي
كُنتُ مِنَ ٱلظَّٰلِمِينَ ٨٧

88. *Fastajabnā lahu wa najjaynahu min al ghammi wa kathalika nunji al muminīn.*

فَٱسۡتَجَبۡنَا لَهُۥ وَنَجَّيۡنَٰهُ
مِنَ ٱلۡغَمِّۚ وَكَذَٰلِكَ نُـۨجِي ٱلۡمُؤۡمِنِينَ ٨٨

8. When Yunus became angry that his people did not respond to his teaching, Allah tested his fidelity within the whale. When engulfed, he cried out to the Lord to confess that he should not have become angry and left his people despite their waywardness.

In the second *raka'ah* after *al-Fatiḥah*: Qur'ān 6:59 *Al-An'ām*:

59. 'And with Him are the keys [to the treasures] of the unseen, none other than He is aware of them, and He alone knows all that is on the land and in the sea. Not a leaf falls without His knowing it and not a grain, in the deepest recess of the earth, be it fresh or desiccated, is not recorded.

Phonetic transliteration
Bismillahir Raḥmānir Raḥīm

بِسْمِ ٱللَّهِ ٱلرَّحْمَٰنِ ٱلرَّحِيمِ

59. *Wa 'indahu mafatiḥul ghaibi la ya'lamuha illa huwa, wa ya'lamu ma fil barri wal baḥri wama tasquṭu min waraqatin illa ya'lamuha, wa la ḥabbatin fi ẓolumatil arḍl wala raṭbin wala yabisin illa fi kitabin mubīn.*

۞ وَعِندَهُۥ مَفَاتِحُ ٱلْغَيْبِ لَا يَعْلَمُهَآ إِلَّا هُوَ ۚ وَيَعْلَمُ مَا فِى
ٱلْبَرِّ وَٱلْبَحْرِ ۚ وَمَا تَسْقُطُ مِن وَرَقَةٍ إِلَّا يَعْلَمُهَا وَلَا حَبَّةٍ
فِى ظُلُمَٰتِ ٱلْأَرْضِ وَلَا رَطْبٍ وَلَا يَابِسٍ إِلَّا فِى كِتَٰبٍ مُّبِينٍ ٥٩

After this, the hands are raised in *qunūt* and the following is recited:

> O Allāh, I beseech you by your Keys to the treasures unseen, to bless Muḥammad and his progeny and to grant me . . . [After stating one's desires one continues] O Allāh, You are my Guardian and Provider and know my desires, so I beseech you, in the names of Muḥammad and his progeny, to grant my request.

Phonetic transliteration
Allāhuma inni as'aluka bi mafatih al ghaib al-lati la ya'lamuha illa ant an tuṣaliya 'ala Muḥammadin wa ālihi wa an . . .

اللهم اني اسئلك بمفاتح الغيب التي لا يعلمها الاانت ان تصلي على
محمد واله وان تفعل بي كذا وكذااااااللهم انت ولي نعمتي والقادر
على طلبتي تعلم حاجتي فاسئلك بحق محمد واله عليه وعليهم
السلام لما قضيتها لي ا

Prayer on the first day of each month

It is recommended to offer the following two *raka'āt* prayers at the start of each month.

The first *rakaʿah*: *Sūrah* 112 — *Al-Tawḥīd* — is recited 30 times after *Al-Fatiḥah.*

The second *rakaʿah*: *Sūrah* 97 — *Al-Qadr* — is recited 30 times after *Al-Fatiḥah.*

AL-TAWḤĪD — MONOTHEISM — ALSO CALLED AL-IKHLĀṢ — SINCERITY — QUR'ĀN 112

In the name of Allāh, the Beneficent, the most Merciful.

1. Say, 'He, Allāh, is Unique,
2. It is upon Allāh that all depend.
3. He fathers none nor has Himself been fathered.
4. And there are none like Him.'

Al-Tawḥīd phonetic transliteration	سُورَةُ الإِخْلَاصِ
Bismillahir Raḥmānir Raḥīm	بِسْمِ اللَّهِ الرَّحْمَٰنِ الرَّحِيمِ
1. *Qul huwa Allāhu aḥad*	قُلْ هُوَ اللَّهُ أَحَدٌ ١
2. *Allāhuṣ ṣamad*	اللَّهُ الصَّمَدُ ٢
3. *Lam yalid wa lam yulad*	لَمْ يَلِدْ وَلَمْ يُولَدْ ٣
4. *Wa lam yakun lahu kufwan aḥad*	وَلَمْ يَكُن لَّهُ كُفُوًا أَحَدٌ ٤

AL-QADR — MEASURE — QUR'ĀN 97

In the name of Allāh, the Beneficent, the most Merciful.

1. We revealed this [Divine Writ] on the Night of Measure,
2. And how may you comprehend the Night of Measure?
3. For the Night of Measure is better than a thousand months,

4. During this night, by Allāh's permission, Angels, and the Spirit, bring down details of every matter,

5. And peace reigns till the break of dawn.

Al-Qadr phonetic transliteration — سُورَةُ القَدْرِ

Bismillahir Raḥmānir Raḥim — بِسْمِ ٱللَّهِ ٱلرَّحْمَٰنِ ٱلرَّحِيمِ

1. *Innā anzalnahu fi laylatil qadr* — إِنَّآ أَنزَلْنَٰهُ فِى لَيْلَةِ ٱلْقَدْرِ ﴿١﴾

2. *Wa ma adraka ma laylatul qadr* — وَمَآ أَدْرَىٰكَ مَا لَيْلَةُ ٱلْقَدْرِ ﴿٢﴾

3. *Laylatul qadri khayrun min alfi shahr* — لَيْلَةُ ٱلْقَدْرِ خَيْرٌ مِّنْ أَلْفِ شَهْرٍ ﴿٣﴾

4. *Tanazzalul malaikatu war ruḥu*
   fiha bi ithni rabihim min kuli amr — تَنَزَّلُ ٱلْمَلَٰٓئِكَةُ وَٱلرُّوحُ فِيهَا بِإِذْنِ رَبِّهِم مِّن كُلِّ أَمْرٍ ﴿٤﴾

5. *Salamun hiya ḥatta maṭlaʿ il fajr.* — سَلَٰمٌ هِىَ حَتَّىٰ مَطْلَعِ ٱلْفَجْرِ ﴿٥﴾

In a narration from Imām Ṣādiq عليه السلام this offers excellent monthly protection.

Prayer offered on ʿĪd Al-Ghadīr

ʿĪd Al-Ghadīr falls on the 18th of Dhul-Hijjah, the day that the Prophet Muḥammad ﷺ announced that Allāh had appointed ʿAlī ibn Abu Ṭalib عليه السلام to be his successor and the first Imām. It is recommended to offer two *rakaʿāt* half an hour prior to noon and to recite in each *rakaʿah: Sūrah Al-Ikhlas* 10 times, *Āyat Al-Kursi* 10 times, and *Sūrah Al-Qadr* 10 times after the recital of *Sūrah Al-Fatiḥah*. It is reported from Imām Ṣādiq عليه السلام that the merit of this prayer equates to the benefits of going on thousands of major and minor pilgrimages and that our desires for this world, or that of the world to come, will be granted.

Prayer for the fulfilment of specific desires

Despite Islamic guidance that every person is responsible for her/his own physical and worldly needs, Muslims are advised also to seek the Lord's help. Here are a few suggestions outlined by the Imāms عليهم السلام.

- To offer two *raka'āt* in the great mosque in Kufa and in each *raka'ah*, to recite *Sūrah* 113, *Sūrah* 114, *Sūrah* 112, *Sūrah* 109, *Sūrah* 110, *Sūrah* 97 and *Sūrah* 87 — after *Sūrah Al-Fatiḥah*. Thereafter to recite the *tasbiḥ* of Lady Faṭimah عليها السلام — '*Allāhu Akbar*' 34 times, '*Al Ḥamdu lilah*' 33 times and '*Subḥana Allāh*' 33 times — before asking for one's requests to be granted.
- Imām 'Ali ibn Al-Ḥusayn عليه السلام advised a frail and financially straitened person to offer two *raka'āt* — to follow that with Allāh's praise and sending the Prophet ﷺ and his progeny عليهم السلام blessings — after which to recite the last three *āyat* of *Sūrah* 59, the first six *āyat* of *Sūrah* 57, and *āyat* 26 and 27 of *Sūrah* 3.[9]

ĀYAT 22, 23, 24 OF SŪRAH 59 — AL-ḤASHR — RESURRECTION

22. He is Allāh, there is no Deity other than Him, the Knower of the seen and the unseen. He is the Beneficent, the Most Merciful.
23. He is Allāh, there is no Deity other than Him, the King (Sovereign), the Holy, the Giver of Peace, the Bestower of Faith, the Overall Controller, the Eminent (Almighty), the Compeller, the Splendid. Allāh is far above anything that they associate with Him.
24. He is Allāh, the Creator, the Originator, the Fashioner, His are All the Most Beautiful Names. All things that are in the heavens and the earth glorify Him. He is the Eminent, the Wise.

Al-Ḥashr Phonetic transliteration

22. *Huwa Allāhu al-lathi la ilaha illa huwa 'alim alghaib wal shahada huwa al-Rahmān al-Rahim.*

هُوَ ٱللَّهُ ٱلَّذِى لَآ إِلَٰهَ إِلَّا هُوَ عَٰلِمُ ٱلْغَيْبِ وَٱلشَّهَٰدَةِ
هُوَ ٱلرَّحْمَٰنُ ٱلرَّحِيمُ ﴿٢٢﴾

9. Many of Allah's Most Beautiful Names appear in these three groups of *āyat*. For a deeper understanding of these and the others refer to pp. 175–246, *The Source of Islamic Spirituality*, Islam in English Press 2004.

23. *Huwa Allāhu al-lathi la ilaha illa huwa al-Malik, al-Quddus, assalam, al-mumin, al-Muhaymin, al-Aziz, al-Jabbār, al-Mutakabir, subhana Allāhi ʿammā yushrikun.*

هُوَ ٱللَّهُ ٱلَّذِي لَآ إِلَٰهَ إِلَّا هُوَ
ٱلۡمَلِكُ ٱلۡقُدُّوسُ ٱلسَّلَٰمُ ٱلۡمُؤۡمِنُ ٱلۡمُهَيۡمِنُ ٱلۡعَزِيزُ
ٱلۡجَبَّارُ ٱلۡمُتَكَبِّرُۚ سُبۡحَٰنَ ٱللَّهِ عَمَّا يُشۡرِكُونَ
٢٣

24. *Huwa Allāhu al-Khaliq, al-Bari', al-Muṣawir lahu al-asma' alhusna, yusabihu lahu mā fi assamāwāti wal arḍ, wa huwa al-Aziz, al-Ḥakim.*

هُوَ ٱللَّهُ ٱلۡخَٰلِقُ ٱلۡبَارِئُ ٱلۡمُصَوِّرُۖ لَهُ ٱلۡأَسۡمَآءُ ٱلۡحُسۡنَىٰۚ
يُسَبِّحُ لَهُۥ مَا فِي ٱلسَّمَٰوَٰتِ وَٱلۡأَرۡضِۖ وَهُوَ ٱلۡعَزِيزُ ٱلۡحَكِيمُ ٢٤

ĀYAT 1—6 OF SŪRAH 57 — AL-ḤADID — IRON

1. All things that are in the heavens and the earth glorify Allāh. He is the Eminent, the Wise.

2. His is the kingdom of heaven and earth, He gives life, brings about death and it is He who has power over all things.

3. He is the First and the Last, the Self-Evident and the Hidden and it is He who has knowledge of all things.

4. It is He who created the heavens and earth over six epochs and then established His authority on the throne (the seat of supreme authority). He knows all that is planted, all that sprouts, everything that descends from the heavens and everything that rises up to it. He is with you wherever you may be and it is He who sees all that you do.

5. His is the kingdom of heaven and earth and all affairs are referred to Allāh.

6. He causes night to replace day and day to replace night and it is He who is aware of all things in all breasts.

Al-Ḥadid phonetic transliteration

1. *Sabbaḥa lilahi ma fi assamāwāti wal arḍ wa huwa al-Aziz al-Ḥakim.*

سَبَّحَ لِلَّهِ مَا فِي ٱلسَّمَٰوَٰتِ وَٱلْأَرْضِ ۖ وَهُوَ ٱلْعَزِيزُ ٱلْحَكِيمُ ١

2. *Lahu mulku assamāwāti wal arḍ yuḥyi wa yumītu wa huwa ʿalā kuli shayin qadīr.*

لَهُۥ مُلْكُ
ٱلسَّمَٰوَٰتِ وَٱلْأَرْضِ ۖ يُحْيِۦ وَيُمِيتُ ۖ وَهُوَ عَلَىٰ كُلِّ شَيْءٍ قَدِيرٌ ٢

3. *Huwa al-awwalu wal ākhiru wal ẓāhiru wal bāṭinu wa huwa bikuli shayin ʿalīm.*

هُوَ ٱلْأَوَّلُ وَٱلْءَاخِرُ وَٱلظَّٰهِرُ وَٱلْبَاطِنُ ۖ وَهُوَ بِكُلِّ شَيْءٍ عَلِيمٌ ٣

4. *Huwa al-lathi khalaqa assamāwāti wal arḍa fi sittati ayām thuma istawā ʿala al-ʿarshi yaʿlamu ma yaliju fi al-arḍi wa ma yukhruju minha wa ma yanzilu min assamā wa ma yaʿruju fiha wa huwa maʿakum ayna ma kuntum wal lahu bima taʿmaluna baṣīr.*

هُوَ ٱلَّذِي خَلَقَ ٱلسَّمَٰوَٰتِ وَٱلْأَرْضَ فِي سِتَّةِ أَيَّامٍ ثُمَّ ٱسْتَوَىٰ
عَلَى ٱلْعَرْشِ ۚ يَعْلَمُ مَا يَلِجُ فِي ٱلْأَرْضِ وَمَا يَخْرُجُ مِنْهَا وَمَا يَنزِلُ مِنَ
ٱلسَّمَآءِ وَمَا يَعْرُجُ فِيهَا ۖ وَهُوَ مَعَكُمْ أَيْنَ مَا كُنتُمْ ۚ وَٱللَّهُ بِمَا تَعْمَلُونَ
بَصِيرٌ ٤

5. *Lahu mulku assamāwāti wal arḍi wa ila Allāhi turjaʿu al umūr.*

لَّهُۥ مُلْكُ ٱلسَّمَٰوَٰتِ وَٱلْأَرْضِ ۚ وَإِلَى ٱللَّهِ تُرْجَعُ ٱلْأُمُورُ ٥

6. *Yuliju al-ayla fi al-nahari wa yuliju al-nahari fi al-ayli wa huwa ʿalimun bithati al-ṣudūr.*

يُولِجُ ٱلَّيْلَ فِي ٱلنَّهَارِ وَيُولِجُ ٱلنَّهَارَ فِي ٱلَّيْلِ ۚ وَهُوَ عَلِيمٌۢ بِذَاتِ
ٱلصُّدُورِ ٦

ĀYAT 26 AND 27 OF SŪRAH 3 — ĀL-IMRĀN — THE FAMILY OF IMRAN

26. Say, 'O Allāh, Owner of the Kingdom, You give kingship to whoever You Like, and it is You who takes kingship from whomever You like. You honour whomever You like and humiliate whomever You like. You hold all things good in Your hand and truly it is You who has power over all things.

27. You cause night to replace day and day to replace night. You raise the living from the dead and the dead from the living and give sustenance without measure to whomever You like.'

Āl-Imrān phonetic transliteration

26. *Qul Allāhuma Mālik al-Mulk tu'ti al-mulka man tashā' wa tanzi'u al-mulka miman tashā' wa tu'izu man tashā', wa tuthillu man tashā', biyadika al-khayru innaka ʿala kuli shayin qadīr.*

قُلِ ٱللَّهُمَّ مَٰلِكَ ٱلْمُلْكِ تُؤْتِى ٱلْمُلْكَ
مَن تَشَآءُ وَتَنزِعُ ٱلْمُلْكَ مِمَّن تَشَآءُ وَتُعِزُّ مَن تَشَآءُ وَتُذِلُّ
مَن تَشَآءُ ۖ بِيَدِكَ ٱلْخَيْرُ ۖ إِنَّكَ عَلَىٰ كُلِّ شَىْءٍ قَدِيرٌ ٢٦

27. *Tuliju al layla fi al-nahari wa tuliju al-nahara fi al layl wa tukhriju al hayya min al mayyit wa tukhriju al mayyit min al hayy wa tarzuqu man tashā'u bighayri hisāb.*

تُولِجُ ٱلَّيْلَ
فِى ٱلنَّهَارِ وَتُولِجُ ٱلنَّهَارَ فِى ٱلَّيْلِ ۖ وَتُخْرِجُ ٱلْحَىَّ مِنَ ٱلْمَيِّتِ
وَتُخْرِجُ ٱلْمَيِّتَ مِنَ ٱلْحَىِّ ۖ وَتَرْزُقُ مَن تَشَآءُ بِغَيْرِ حِسَابٍ ٢٧

Imām ʿAlī ibn al-Husayn ﷷ said that after reciting the above, Allāh will grant your desires for this world and for the world to come.

It is reported from Imām ʿAlī ﷷ that a four-rakaʿāt prayer should be offered to invoke Allāh to grant desires

In the first *rakaʿah a*fter *Al-Fatiḥah*, to recite Qur'ān 3:173 (*Āl-ʿImrān*) seven times — 'Allāh is sufficient for us, He who protects us is Most Excellent.'

Phonetic transliteration
Bismillahir Raḥmānir Raḥim

بِسْمِ ٱللَّهِ ٱلرَّحْمَٰنِ ٱلرَّحِيمِ

173. *Ḥasbuna Allāhu wa niʿmal wakīl*

حَسْبُنَا ٱللَّهُ وَنِعْمَ ٱلْوَكِيلُ ١٧٣

In the second *rakaʿah a*fter *Al-Fatiḥah*, to recite the following *āyah* of *Al-Kahf* seven times, 'Everything is as Allāh wills, there is no power other than Allāh's. If you see me as less than you in wealth and children . . . ' (Qur'ān 18:39).

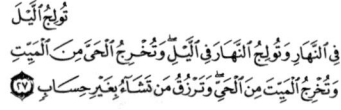

Phonetic transliteration
Bismillahir Raḥmānir Raḥim

بِسْمِ ٱللَّهِ ٱلرَّحْمَٰنِ ٱلرَّحِيمِ

39. *Ma shāa Allāhu la quwata illa billah, in tarani ana aqalla minka mālan wa waladā . . .*

وَلَوْلَآ إِذْ
دَخَلْتَ جَنَّتَكَ قُلْتَ مَا شَآءَ ٱللَّهُ لَا قُوَّةَ إِلَّا بِٱللَّهِ ۚ إِن تَرَنِ أَنَا۠
أَقَلَّ مِنكَ مَالًا وَوَلَدًا ٣٩

In the third *raka*ʿ*ah* after *Al-Fatiḥah*, to recite the following *āyah* seven times, ‘There is no Divinity other than You — limitless Glory beyond imperfection. Truly I was among the unjust . . .’ (Qur’ān 21:87).

In the fourth *raka*ʿ*ah* after *Al–Fatiḥah*, to recite the following *āyah* seven times, ‘I entrust my affairs to Allāh, truly Allāh watches over His servants’ (Qur’ān 40:440).

Phonetic transliteration
Bismillahir Raḥmānir Raḥim

بِسْمِ ٱللَّهِ ٱلرَّحْمَٰنِ ٱلرَّحِيمِ

44. *Wa ufawwiḍu amri ila Allāh, inna Allāha baṣīrun bil* ʿ*ibād.*

فَسَتَذْكُرُونَ مَآ أَقُولُ لَكُمْ ۚ وَأُفَوِّضُ أَمْرِىٓ إِلَى
ٱللَّهِ ۚ إِنَّ ٱللَّهَ بَصِيرٌۢ بِٱلْعِبَادِ ٤٤

He said that after reciting the above, Allāh will grant your desires for this world and for the world to come.

Prayer for istikhārah

The word *istikhārah* — to petition Allāh for guidance to all that is good — is derived from the Arabic root word *khair* — good. Human beings, created with intelligence and the ability to reason, are well equipped to evaluate the benefits and disadvantages of actions and make informed decisions. However, at moments of stress, or when obliged to make decisions crucial to their future success, believers are advised to seek the guidance of Allāh — Knower of All that is Hidden and Manifest — to direct them to the ‘best’ solution via *istikhārah*.

- Scholars have dedicated chapters, even volumes, to this subject. The most famous work is the book of Al-Sayyid ibn Ṭawus (d. 664 AH)

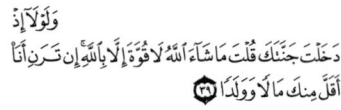

'*Fatḥ al-Abwāb*' (Opening the Doors) in which he records 20 different approaches to the seeking of *istikhārah*[10]

- Shaykh Saduq refers to Imām Ṣādiq ﵇ saying, 'When one wishes to consult Allāh, pray two *rakaʿāt*, praise Allāh, send blessings to the Prophet ﷺ and his progeny and then say, "O Allāh if this action is beneficial in terms of religion or worldly matters, please make it easy for me to under-take; if it is not, please erase it from my thoughts."' The narrator asked the Imām ﵇ which *sūrahs* should be recited in the *rakaʿāt* and was told that both *Sūrah Al-Ikhlas* Qur'ān 112 and *Sūrah Al-Kāfirūn* Qur'ān 109 should be recited in the knowledge that the Prophet ﷺ said that the recitation of *Al-Ikhlas* is equal to the recitation of one-third of the Qur'ān. **Wasa'il al-Shiʿah, Vol. 8, p. 66**

10. It is reported in a *ḥadīth* of the Holy Prophet ﷺ that the paths to Allāh Almighty are equivalent to the 'breath of all creatures'. This illustrates that there are a never-ending variety of ways in which to communicate with one's Lord.